REVELATION

THE END TIMES AND THE NEVER REACHED

CHRIS L. CARTER

ASSEMBLIES OF GOD WORLD MISSIONS
Springfield, Missouri

Assemblies of God World Missions
1445 N. Boonville Avenue
Springfield, MO 65802-1894

Printed in the United States of America

24 23 22 21 20   1 2 3 4 5

ISBN 978-1-7356545-0-8

CONTENTS

FOREWORD

I AM SOMETIMES ASKED, "What is the Lord saying to us in this time?" I believe this short book by Dr. Chris Carter answers that question.

Through the lens of Revelation 7:9–12, he opens the entire book in plain words, easy to understand, probing in their application.

Chris understands Revelation as I have always understood it: that the book is not a riddle to be deciphered, but a message to believers of all generations to be faithful to Christ's mission in the face of suffering and trial. In fact, the songs of Revelation—especially Revelation 7:9–12—give us a chance to sing the songs of heaven during our sojourn here; it's music piped down to us from above.

The book of Revelation, as Dr. Carter shows, asks us this fundamental question: "Will we stay committed to the mission when it will cost us our money, our homes, and our lives?" The first century believers were asked to answer this question, and so must we.

Let me digress with a personal story. I was a young pastor in California. Mother's Day approached and I chose to preach a sermon on not being afraid of the times—that if Amram and Jochebed had been afraid of the times, the world would never have had Moses. And, without Moses, we would not have had the first five books of the Bible or the deliverance of Israel from bondage. I encouraged the congregation to not fear in the turbulent times we lived in.

A married couple listened to me that day, Mark and Jane. Jane was a paraplegic, permanently confined to a wheelchair because of a horrendous accident when she was a teenager. They had decided not to have children because of her condition. I did not know this at the time. After they left church and went home, they talked and prayed—they decided to let their faith guide them and not their fears. The result was two children born to them—the first, a girl named Lindsey—who would become the wife of Dr. Christopher Carter and the mother to their three children. Mark and Jane have never been missionaries—but they stayed missional and passed that on to their daughter and grandchildren.

Writing from a deep well of scholarship and personal experience, this book reminds us in these uncertain and difficult times about what the book of Revelation is really all about. It, in Chris' words, "challenges us to change the way we live, to alter our behavior and bring it into conformity with His character. In short, reading Revelation should change the way we do absolutely everything."

This book doesn't take long to read, but its impact will last a very long time in your life. I encourage you to soak its message into your heart and life.

Dr. George O. Wood
Chairman, World Assemblies of God Fellowship

EDITOR'S PREFACE

TWENTY-TWENTY CREATED unprecedented challenges. Globally, we each carry our own pandemic story. Some tragic tales of loss, others devastating economic challenges. Our stories drive the question. How do we live when the world falls apart?

Caught mid-trip in international travel by the pandemic we found ourselves marooned far from home, separated from our daughter by ten thousand miles, homeless, without transportation, with only one week's change of clothing and a few electronics. We hunkered down in a church fellowship hall in an inner city and watched our world unravel at a rapidly accelerating pace. Exposed to COVID we dared not meet with friends or family. Ultimately, we contracted the virus and weathered the storm.

The story is still being written for the COVID-19 pandemic. History will tell if we overreacted to a passing inconvenience or were blindsided by a multi-year catastrophe on a global scale. Writing and living in the middle of the story it's impossible to know. The daily challenges obscure the big picture.

Revelation, and Chris Carter's study of this book provide critical answers in a time of swirling uncertainty. How do we live in unprecedented times? We base our lives on the future God promises rather than the fears of the present.

Revelation: The End Times and the Never Reached draws us into the throne room of heaven. Revealing the grand cosmic scheme of time and eternity, it gives the necessary perspective to make sense of a chaotic world.

In Asia Pacific Missions our mission is to plant the church everywhere it is not. Our priority is the never reached. These are the peoples of the world who have not only never heard the gospel in their lifetime or in past generations but in all of human history. This book and others like it are intended to draw the Church's attention to the never reached.

I pray as you read this book, the Bold Song of Victory and the Humble Song of Praise become the soundtrack of your life. When faced with the question, *Will we stay committed to mission when it will cost us our money, our homes, and our lives?* Your answer will be a bold and unqualified, Yes!

Bryan Webb
Pacific Oceania Area Director,
Assemblies of God USA World Missions

AUTHOR'S PREFACE

I AM A NEW TESTAMENT SCHOLAR, well versed in biblical and modern research languages and quite capable of writing detailed studies on fascinating topics related to my discipline that no one except my fellow scholars would understand or appreciate. This is not that kind of book! If you are interested in a carefully documented and tightly argued exegesis of Revelation, may I suggest that you consult the excellent commentaries by David Aune and G. K. Beale, or one of the many monographs that are available. This book has only a few footnotes, and while my viewpoint *is* defensible, I have not defended it in a way that would satisfy any critical New Testament scholar. Let me assure you that this is quite intentional. I am writing for the broadest possible audience, and I do not want to lose anyone in the minutiae of sorting out my rationale for every interpretative turn which the careful reader will no doubt be able to detect. The reader should also understand that I am not claiming to be the first to have detected or emphasized mission in Revelation, but I do hope that my presentation will be found to be fresh and unique.

Two further notes: first, I often refer to the western church or western forms of Christianity. I do so from the perspective of one who has spent many years living in both the United States and the United Kingdom. I often speak in generalities and sometimes even stereotypes. One must recognize the necessity of doing so when addressing the big picture of any subject, but equally we must acknowledge that such tools by their nature neglect the multiple exceptions to observed patterns. Second, all of the translations of Revelation are my own from the Nestle Aland 28th edition of the Greek New Testament. I have not consulted modern English versions of the New Testament.

Revelation has generated no shortage of varying interpretations over the centuries, and I have no illusions about being the first to come up with one that convinces everyone. But I do pray that this book with its foray into the missions message of Revelation will spark missional thinking and more importantly, missional living.

C.L.C.

July 2020

ACKNOWLEDGMENTS

THIS BOOK HAS BEEN more than ten years in the making. It began with my family itinerating to become missionaries to Japan. At the time, we had just completed our first term in the Philippines where we had served at Asia Pacific Theological Seminary. During our time in the Philippines, we sensed God's clear leading to Japan. However, the transfer of fields did not come easily. In the same week that we said, "yes" to God about Japan, my wife, Lindsey, was diagnosed with a heart problem, and our daughter, Adelaide, was diagnosed with juvenile arthritis. On top of this, our supervisor did not grant us permission to switch fields to Japan. At the same time, the churches in which we were ministering found themselves in the aftermath of the Great Recession.

As we traveled around the U.S. raising our missionary budget and facing many trials and discouragements, I felt like the Lord was leading me to preach about the message of missions that features prominently in the book of Revelation, but often finds no hearing. It seemed to be a message that precisely fit the depressed and apocalyptic mood of the American church at the time. And it was a message I needed to hear myself! Along the way, pastors and congregants kept approaching me after services with excitement saying that they had never heard anything like that before and also expressing their thankfulness for the timely encouragement brought to them by the message. Then, several pastors asked me if I would consider putting these ideas into book form. Finally, I sat down and started writing, and I eventually submitted the manuscript to a publisher. Even though the book was accepted for publication, I didn't have peace about publishing it, so I just held on to the manuscript.

Nine years later as I was worshipping in the church we pastor in Japan, Tsukuba International Christian Assembly, God spoke to me. He said, "send the Revelation book to Bryan Webb." In response, I wrote one of those "Excuse me for sending this strange message . . . but" kind of e-mails. Bryan liked the book, but didn't know what to do with it, so he put it on the back burner. However, when the pandemic struck in the spring of 2020, he felt like the moment for this message had come. Eventually, our Asia Pacific Regional Director, Jeff Hartensveld, became convinced that God had orchestrated the timing of this book coming to light. And the team in the AP office has worked tirelessly to see this project through to completion. I am deeply grateful to Jeff Hartensveld, Bryan Webb, Leslie Thomas, Nicco Musacchio, Elish Tram, and all the people working behind the scenes in the AP office for their encouragement and hard work that has made this book possible.

Because this project has such a long history, I have a huge debt of gratitude owed to hundreds of people. Many friends read earlier drafts of the book and made helpful comments. My family listened to countless iterations of the sermon version of this material. And multiple pastor friends encouraged me to write something like this. You all know who you are, and even though I can't list your names, I do express to you my heartfelt thanks.

REVELATION

THE END TIMES AND THE NEVER REACHED

INTRODUCTION

EVERYWHERE ONE TURNS these days, surreal phrases like "the new normal," "unprecedented," "economic collapse," and "pandemic" assault the senses. It feels like walking through a carnival funhouse filled with mirrors distorting reality till down looks like up and up looks like down. This has left many Christians feeling the once clear path leading to the future has become a black box containing equal parts fear and mystery. In this new world rocked by uncertainty, many Christians are turning to the end of the Bible to find answers.

Many people have the idea that Revelation is very difficult to understand. In a sense, this is quite true. Although the images and symbols of Revelation do pose a daunting problem for interpretation, Revelation as a whole has a clear and understandable message. However, in our human tendency to get distracted by bright shinny things, we often get so taken with the mysterious minutia of Revelation that we miss the big picture.

All one has to do is scroll through Facebook to find well-intentioned believers trying to correlate the events surrounding the worldwide coronavirus pandemic with the proper chapter of Revelation. I can't tell you how many times I have been asked if this crisis is the beginning of the end. Is this the tribulation about which Revelation warns? Is the handwriting of Armageddon on the wall?

Beyond the plague sweeping across the globe, our world seems to be more politically polarized than at any other time in living memory. The nations of the world have lost the will to cooperate and are pursuing their own agendas in a way that seems destined to end in conflict, with nation rising against nation. Domestically, racial tensions have soared to the breaking point, and a culture war rages dividing neighbor against neighbor. This division penetrates even into our homes, to the point that fathers and sons and mothers and daughters can't agree on what is right and wrong. In America today, landmark court cases and legislative agendas give us reason to question whether our long-cherished religious freedoms may be on their way out. Are we now walking the road Jesus had in mind when He said, "Brother will betray brother to the point of death, and father his own child also. And children will rise up against their parents, and they will be put to death" (Mark 13:12)?

In a sense, the Church has been posing this question regularly now for more than two millennia. Like us, in times of uncertainty and distress, our forefathers and foremothers felt compelled to ask an all-important question: *What time is it?* In other words, in God's plan for the universe and His Church, which culminates with the return of Christ, where and when are we? In whatever way we choose to answer this question, it is certain many Christians have the feeling Jesus' return can't be far off. Consequently, more and more attention is being paid to questions about the end times. In particular, more and more people have been turning to the book of Revelation and its vivid and mysterious unveiling of the end.

As a career missionary to Japan, nothing excites me more than the prospect of the Church of Jesus Christ setting its gaze unblinkingly on the end of times and the book of Revelation. I am firmly convinced Revelation was given to the Church for such a time as this. God gave it to us as a big, red reset button for hard times. Twenty-twenty seems to be a moment in time when we need to go ahead and break the glass and push the button. This book is an invitation to do so.

Before we push the button together, allow me to make a small disclaimer. When you push Revelation's big, red reset button, *do not* expect COVID-19 or whatever other monstrous beast happens to be destroying your life at the moment to disappear. That's not how this works! Revelation's reset is not about resetting the world. It is about resetting us! Revelation resets our perspective by calling us individually and collectively out of misplaced priorities and fears and back to the heart of God, back to mission.

> *Twenty-twenty seems to be a moment in time when we need to go ahead and break the glass and push the button. This book is an invitation to do so.*

Speaking of mission, in the following pages, the words *mission, missional,* and *missions* appear regularly. In most cases, I employ these words in a very broad sense. *Missions* involves the response of the Church to Christ's command to proclaim the good news that salvation is found in Jesus to the whole world. Under its umbrella, one finds churches and individuals who send missionaries, the institutions which train missionaries, and the churches and organizations missionaries build around the globe. *Missional*, in turn, speaks of a way of life that embraces missions.

Missional people may, in some cases, never leave their countries of origin; however, these people and the organizations in which they labor make decisions, use resources, and in short, do everything with the single-minded purpose of preaching Jesus to the world. The book of Revelation can be called missional insofar as it seeks to form communities of just this sort of people. Like *missions* and *missional*, *mission* fits into the same constellation of ideas, but it focuses more specifically on the goal of all activities and attitudes related to missions, namely, lost people entering into relationship with Christ.

In this little book, I am not trying to unveil all the mysteries of Revelation. No one can do so. In fact, I am only setting out to explain four verses: Revelation 7:9–12. However, dear reader, in spite of the modesty of our journey together, the rewards of completing it are grand. For to understand these verses is to understand the book of Revelation, and to understand the book of Revelation is to have your entire world reimagined, redefined, and rebirthed by the God who spoke the universe into being with a word.

Before we begin this intrepid voyage into what seems to many the dark, scary, and unknown recesses of the Word of God, we have to get ourselves into the right frame of mind. We must understand what sort of words we will meet in the pages of Revelation, and most importantly, we must understand what sort of people first read and understood these words. Only by doing this at the outset will we be in a position for the life-changing power of these words written by John so long ago to accomplish their intended purpose.

WHAT SORT OF WORDS?

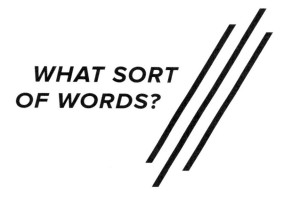

IF WE WANT to talk about what sort of words we meet in the book of Revelation, we must start with the four verses about which our particular adventure is concerned: Revelation 7:9–12.

> After I saw these things, behold, there was a great crowd, which no one was capable of counting, from every nation and tribe and people and tongue standing before the throne and before the Lamb, having been clothed with white flowing robes and holding palm branches in their hands. And they keep on crying out in a loud voice, saying:
>> Salvation be to our God, who sits upon the throne, and to the Lamb!

And all the angels who had stood surrounding the throne and
the elders and the four living creatures also fell before the throne
upon their faces, and they worshipped God, saying:
> *It's true!*
> *Blessing and glory and wisdom and thanksgiving and honor*
> *and power and might be to our God forever and ever!*
> *It's true!*

Here we find deceptively brief and simple words. Despite such apparent simplicity, however, some New Testament scholars have called this passage the most difficult in the entire book of Revelation. Arguably, Revelation is the most difficult book in the whole Bible to understand. So, these words may well be the hardest words in all of Scripture.

Now you are beginning to see why these four verses are not for the fainthearted Bible reader! One of the things making these words so difficult to understand has to do with the sort of words we encounter throughout John's apocalypse. Somewhat uniquely, Revelation combines three kinds or genres of writing into one presentation, and this combination lies behind the headaches many Christians seem to get when they read the Apocalypse. So, let's look briefly at these three kinds of writing.

The first sort of writing one meets in Revelation won't be a surprise at all. Of course, it's prophecy. Everyone knows Revelation and prophecy go hand in hand. However, not everyone has a correct understanding of what exactly makes prophecy—prophecy. At its heart, prophecy does not necessarily have anything to do with foretelling future events; rather, it fundamentally concerns itself with the forth-telling of the Word of God. In other words, prophecy has more to do with preaching than predicting. Now, don't get me wrong. Revelation does have much to say about future events, and generations of Christians have rightly recognized this fact. Nonetheless, many times, the future looms so large in discussions of Revelation we cannot hear the sermon spoken to us here and now, calling us not to speculation about what will be but to repentance and a life-changing response to the proclaimed Word of God.

Beyond prophecy, another sort of writing lies in wait for us in the pages of Revelation—the dark and misunderstood stranger of apocalyptic literature. It would be foolhardy to attempt a full explanation of apocalypticism, apocalyptic eschatology, apocalyptic literature, apocalypse, and the like here. Complicated debates continue to rage on all of these subjects. For our purposes, we need to understand, first of all, an apocalypse is unlike any modern book or movie within our experience. It conveys meanings in ways the modern or postmodern reader cannot understand without becoming familiar with the rules of the story. This, however, is not the place for yet another tome on that subject. What you really need to know is that apocalypses are for really, really, really bad times. Ancient Middle Eastern people only resorted to this bizarre form of writing when all political, economic, and spiritual hope seemed lost. Sound familiar?

An apocalypse does not communicate its message merely through words, sentences, and paragraphs. Rather, the message comes in the form of word pictures, often loaded with social and cultural meaning, very difficult for us to understand today. One pastor I know calls this "special-effects writing." Writing that functions like special effects in the movies: the visuals, not the words, tell the story. Ultimately, anyone who wants to understand Revelation must grasp its strange "pictures" tell us that in spite of our seemingly hopeless political, economic, and spiritual situation, our God, Yahweh, remains in control of the course of history. He will take His people to a place of absolute victory.

So, we know Revelation is prophecy and apocalypse, but it is also a letter. That's right. Revelation unfolds just like any other letter in the New Testament. You may not have noticed it, but this letter actually begins in a way anyone who has opened a mailbox will readily recognize. Indeed, verse 4 contains precisely the same information appearing on nearly every envelope you have ever pulled from your mailbox. On a snail-mail letter, you will find the name of the sender in the upper left-hand corner of the envelope, and you will find the name of the addressee near the center. I want to take just a minute to ponder the "envelope" into which John stuffed the letter of Revelation so many years ago. Take a look at chapter 1, verse 4:

When we read Revelation, we have actually opened a very old piece of mail addressed to someone else.

John to the seven churches which are in Asia ...

When we read Revelation, we have actually opened a very old piece of mail addressed to someone else. In this case, John intended churches in Asia Minor to read his letter. Often, we read Revelation without realizing we are reading over the shoulders of our distant brothers and sisters of first-century Asia Minor. In practical terms, this means we cannot really understand the message until we can read it through their eyes—comprehending not only what its words would have meant to them but also how its words would have made them feel.

How can we possibly bridge the gulf of centuries, language, culture, and circumstances separating us from them? The short answer? We can never do so completely. Nonetheless, we must step into their shoes as much as possible, if we would hear the words of Revelation as they were meant to be heard. In the next chapter, we will try to put ourselves in the place of first-century Asia Minor Christians and to hear the Apocalypse as they would have heard it.

TIME TRAVEL

AS WE TRAVEL back in time and enter the world of the Christians living in first-century Asia Minor, we find ourselves in the midst of a crisis in mission worthy of an apocalypse. John addresses the nature of this crisis in the short letters his heavenly guide commands him to write to the seven churches of Asia Minor (Rev. 2–3). Although I have rarely heard it from a pulpit, in recent commentaries and monographs, New Testament scholars have become increasingly aware the entire letter of Revelation has missions at its very heart.

This letter really concerns itself with one thing from beginning to end, God's mission to save the world from the power of sin and death and the Church's call to join Him in this mission through gospel preaching and living. What we see in the letters to the seven churches reveals the precise dimensions of a mounting crisis in mission. So, at the very beginning of Revelation, John places missions squarely at the core of His message to the Church.

Looking briefly at each letter, one realizes God's messenger pronounces the Almighty's evaluation of each church according to its commitment to missions. Ultimately, each church will either stand or fall depending on its ability to remain missional under difficult circumstances.

The first letter addresses the church in the city of Ephesus. The church in Ephesus receives praise because they know the gospel well enough to detect and reject the false apostles in their midst. Even as John wrote to them, they were doing well in rejecting the false teaching of the Nicolaitans. The Ephesian believers receive further praise because they have suffered for the name of Jesus and have not grown weary in the midst of suffering. In other words, they know the gospel, and they are willing to live it and proclaim it even when doing so results in painful suffering.

However, in spite of their glorious past and present, the church in Ephesus stands in danger of judgment because of their waning commitment in the face of continued suffering for the sake of the gospel. Their formerly radical and unwavering commitment to the gospel is "the first love" to which they must return or face divine judgment. Beyond this stern warning of judgment, the letter to Ephesus draws attention to the rich rewards of single-minded, unflinching, radical commitment to continuous missional living—eating from the tree of life in God's paradise (Rev. 2:7).

In Smyrna, we also become acquainted with a suffering church. For them, mission has produced, on one hand, material poverty, and on the other hand, spiritual wealth. As an added bonus, the letter promises this church increased suffering and imprisonment, presumably because of gospel preaching and living. In all of this, John exhorts them to stay committed to mission, to the point of death, with the promise that God will give them the crown of life if they remain faithful (Rev. 2:10).

The church in Pergamum lives in a rough neighborhood — one "where Satan has his throne" (Rev. 2:13 NIV). Here the church is "holding fast" to the name of Jesus in the face of martyrdom (Rev. 2:13). They are doing well in being committed to mission, but they are in danger because of idolatry and false teaching. As we will see later, idolatry and false teaching most likely relate to a relaxing of the gospel message to make preaching it less dangerous. The letter warns swift judgment awaits the church compromising the gospel for the sake of its own comfort and safety.

The believers in Thyatira have a solid commitment to mission including works of love, faithfulness, endurance, and service. Nonetheless, they too are facing issues of idolatry and sexual immorality, which have the power to destroy them and their witness. Although some of them have been entrapped by these deadly temptations, a minority has remained faithful. The angel gives John a message of encouragement for them. They must hold fast and persevere in mission and thereby receive the reward reserved for the faithful in the end.

Strong words greet those in Sardis. They have a reputation for being alive, but this appearance is a smokescreen. We soon learn the true state of affairs. Although they possess a lively exterior, the members of the church in Sardis are corpses on the inside. Their act has not deceived God; He knows! As an antidote to death, the church must remember what they received and heard. What they received and heard was the gospel through which God had saved them and commissioned them to proclaim the truth to their neighbors.

Their living death had come about when they, under social pressure, severed the tie between the saving work of the gospel and the charge to proclaim it. Whenever and wherever Christians try to hold onto faith while jettisoning mission, they become zombies. At first glance, they seem to be moving and alive, but on closer inspection, they have no real life within them. In such a situation, only one thing will save the church in Sardis from a grim existence as the walking dead. They must return to the gospel.

They must re-embrace both the faith and the proclamation intrinsic to it. Thus, through John, Yahweh commands the church in Sardis to keep to the gospel (Rev. 3:3). In other words, in order to truly live again, the zombie church in Sardis must return to its roots and become a missional church—one committed to preaching and living the gospel to the point of death. Nonetheless, there are some in Sardis who have not abandoned this mission, and they will receive the promise of having their names remain in the Book of Life. Furthermore, God promises He himself will finally clothe in pure white garments those in Sardis who persist in living missional lives.

In Philadelphia, the church has "little power" (Rev. 3:8). The Greek word used here, *dunamis*, refers to socioeconomic status, and the context further indicates their lack of power and status comes directly from their faithfulness to the gospel and refusal to deny the name of Jesus. In short, the church in Philadelphia continues to be missional even when it costs them their money and social status. For their endurance and faithfulness, God promises them deliverance from coming temptation and a glorious future in the New Jerusalem.

Perhaps better known than any of the other churches, the congregation in Laodicea has a tepid version of Christianity. God ardently desires they would instead remain hot or cold, but in their present state, they stand in danger of becoming divine spit. ("In this way because you are lukewarm and neither hot nor cold,

I am about to spit you out from my mouth" Rev. 3:16). Many times, interpreters have the mistaken notion that being hot or cold refers to being saved or not saved. However, such an understanding fails to deal with the fact that in this passage, God views both hot and cold states as desirable. He is not willing any should perish and does not long for the people He loves to be eternally lost rather than serving Him half-heartedly.

The context of the letter makes clear that hot and cold have to do with the deeds of the Laodiceans and what those deeds say about them. It doesn't make much sense for God to say, "I wish your deeds were really good or really bad, but as it is, they are just so-so." What does the enigmatic hot and cold metaphor really signify? The answer comes only when we consider both the geography and economy of Laodicea.

First-century Laodicea lay in the Lycus river valley, with its neighboring towns of Colossae and Hierapolis at higher elevations. Although the inhabitants of Laodicea had built their town near a river and therefore a source of fresh water, the river had a tendency to dry up in the hottest and driest parts of the year. As a result, it became necessary to find an alternative source of fresh water, and engineers designed and built two aqueducts from the higher hill cities of Colossae and Hierapolis.

Colossae was well known for its springs of fresh, cool mineral water believed by some to have medicinal value. Hierapolis was known for its hot springs, and travelers would come from far and wide to enjoy their healing properties and rest their road-weary bodies in the soothing hot water. However, as the cool waters of Colossae made their journey to Laodicea, they warmed, losing their refreshing cool properties. Similarly, by the time the hot spring water of Hierapolis arrived in Laodicea, it had cooled and was no different than the water from Colossae. Both had become lukewarm. Not only was the water tepid, but ancient accounts tell us the stone with which the builders had constructed the aqueduct made the water taste bad. Yuck! Just thinking about it makes you understand why someone might want to spit out such water.

The metaphor of lukewarm water made a lot of sense to the church in Laodicea. They lived with it every day. As we read this text in the modern world, most of the time, the point sails clean over our heads. You see, whereas the waters of Colossae and Hierapolis were sources of commercial success for their cities, the water of Laodicea only brought it poverty.

Imagine you're a weary trader traveling thousands of miles by camel caravan. You're thinking to yourself, "I could stop in Colossae and have a nice drink from their cool mineral spring. Maybe it would even heal this nasty rash. On the other hand, the hot springs in Hierapolis do sound lovely. How I would like to soak my tired, achy body in their hot water." It would be an odd traveler indeed who would pass up cold water or a nice hot bath for the hot, dry, dusty town of Laodicea with its terrible-tasting, lukewarm water. Not even the fanciest billboard would make someone go to Laodicea rather than Colossae or Hierapolis.

The difference between hot or cold water and lukewarm water lies in the usefulness of the former as sources of refreshment and healing and the comparative uselessness of the latter. Indeed, because Laodicea had this undesirable water, they could not attract as many travelers or as much business as their neighbors. However, the city was not poor.

At the time when John wrote Revelation, the city was still recovering from a devastating earthquake which had struck around AD 60. Had they been poor, they could not have rebuilt the city. Far from being poor, the Laodiceans were rich, and they thought that their riches spoke eloquently of their spiritual success. However,

Jesus gives them quite a shock when He lets them know their true state. In spite of their inflated self-esteem, they are in actual fact poor, blind, and naked.

This description drips with irony. The Laodiceans had made their money from an eye medicine that cured blindness and from black wool from which clothes were made. The church had exploited these sources of wealth and had become rich. However, physical wealth had led to spiritual poverty. Most likely the church had compromised with idol worship in order to partici-pate in the economy of their city. They had worshipped idols and the emperor, and under social pressure, they had stopped sharing the gospel. Thus, they became wealthy, but at a great cost. Jesus' letter to the Laodiceans warns us against a problem that many in the Church still have today. Many believe that financial success corresponds to spiritual success.

Many famous American television evangelists propagate this notion—teaching that financial success and spiritual success invariably go together. The Laodiceans would agree, but Jesus does not. In the case of the Laodiceans, He says, "do not think your financial success evidences your spiritual success! Although you have money, you are spiritually wretched, pitiable, naked, blind, and poor!" Jesus doesn't pull any punches! But don't worry, Jesus does give them a way out. In verse 18, He supplies the solution to their problem. *I advise you to buy from me gold which has been refined by fire in order that you might be rich. I also advise you to buy white garments in order that you may be clothed and not expose the shame of your nakedness. Furthermore, I advise you to anoint your eyes with eye salve in order that you might see* (Rev. 3:18).

They had abandoned their mission. Abandoning their mission left them wretched, pitiable, poor, blind, and naked. Notice, being naked represents the exact opposite condition of the faithful

19

preachers of the gospel who will receive white robes as a reward for their gospel labors. As with the other churches in Asia Minor, we find in Laodicea a church struggling with mission, and God desperately longs for them to return to productive labor in this area. He desires nothing less than for Laodicea to be a church preaching Christ — healing cold water and hot soothing water to the weary nations.

We have spent some time looking at these seven churches because doing so reveals the agony of the first readers of Revelation as they struggled with being a missional church. Lest we too quickly judge our spiritual ancestors as immature Christians unable to embrace the missional zeal of modern evangelical Christians, we need to appreciate the social, economic, and historical environment that made missions such a difficult choice for these early believers.

In those days, a tyrannical despot by the name of Domitian sat on the throne of the Roman Empire, and in terms of sheer evil, he would have given even Hitler a run for his money. Suetonius, who was born just a few years after the apostle Paul, fills in the picture of Domitian's detestable character, depicting him as sexually perverse, cruel, and greedy. He also mentions the particular disdain and mercilessness with which Domitian dealt with Jews and Christians, whom he viewed as one group.

Under Domitian, the church experienced its first widespread and fairly systematic persecution. The flashpoint for much of this persecution had to do with emperor worship. Emperor worship had been part and parcel of imperial rule since Julius Caesar, but Domitian became obsessed with the idea of his divinity to an extent that set him quite apart from other emperors. His obsession led him to demand even those usually exempted from emperor worship be forced to worship him on pain of torture, seizure of property, exile, and death. But emperor worship did not primarily have to do with religion.

In Roman times, the emperor cult represented the patriotic glue holding the empire together. There were so many gods and religions in the first-century Greco-Roman world that no one could possibly keep them straight. In the midst of this religious pluralism and chaos, emperor worship provided a unifying symbol and quasi-religious experience—uniting an otherwise disconnected population. In modern terms, emperor worship has more in common with the American flag than statues of Buddha. In other words, the goal was patriotism rather than sincere belief.

To refuse to worship the emperor would, in our modern American terms, be to defile the star-spangled banner by rubbing it in the dirt followed by a public flag-burning ceremony. Many Americans would be shocked at such unpatriotic behavior; social media would label them malefactors, ingrates, un-American, and so on. In the Roman world, the consequences for unpatriotic behavior had more teeth than simple outrage or public scorn, and the Christians of Asia Minor were facing these consequences on multiple fronts. They were paying the price for their unpatriotic refusal to worship Domitian.

One of the most striking areas in which the churches of Asia Minor would have been feeling the pinch of persecution was their wallets. We know from ancient sources that cities in Asia Minor would have been keen to demonstrate their loyalty to the emperor and their Roman patriotism. They built temples to emperors and scrupulously enforced emperor worship, all in the hope of gaining favor with Rome. Such favor would bring new buildings, special rights, citizenship, commerce, and countless other benefits. Consequently, they were desperate to avoid even the hint of rebellion or an unpatriotic attitude.

In these cities, laborers participated in an ancient version of the trade union. They had formed guilds, and it was impossible to practice many trades without being a member of a guild. The avid Bible reader will perhaps recall reading about the Ephesian silver workers' trade guild in the book of Acts. While ministering in Ephesus, the apostle Paul narrowly escaped from the hands of rioters whom the guild had stirred up (Acts 19:23–41). To participate in the trade guild, one had to worship both the emperor and any patron deities the trade guild adopted. Trade guild meetings also featured meals of meat sacrificed to idols and idolatrous ceremonies.

Beyond the lower-class artisans and laborers who would have been involved in trade guilds, the more socially affluent would have faced financial and social difficulties related to their Christian faith. Anyone serious about becoming successful in business would have had to build and nurture relationships with the upper classes. The social occasions on which one made such business contacts, negotiated with clients, and appeased contractors all revolved around idolatrous worship and moral depravity. Many times, such business happened at pagan temples as guests gathered in the temple dining rooms and ate food sacrificed to pagan gods. At other times, these discussions happened around the reclining tables of Roman villas.

These types of parties usually involved practices that would make the most oversexed and desensitized-to-violence modern person blush. The guests overindulged in food until they could eat no more; then they would visit the vomitorium, purge themselves, and return to the banquet to experience the pleasure of eating all over again. There would be excessive drinking and drunkenness. Then the so-called "after-dinners" followed.

Traveling bands of dancing prostitutes would be contracted for the really "good" parties, and following the meals, they would dance. In the midst of this, the dining guests would participate in a drunken orgy with the prostitutes. (Notice the church in Thyatira fails at these very points, i.e., eating food sacrificed to idols and indulging in sexual immorality [Rev. 2:20].) This was not a fringe practice but normal behavior for that time. Anyone who wanted to be successful in business would have had to attend such gatherings from time to time, and the wealthy would have been expected to attend such gatherings in order to maintain their social standing.

In this context, it should come as no surprise the two most repeated themes in the book of Revelation have to do with finances and idolatry. Remember those who make it to the end, who wear the white robes, and who have their names written in the Book of Life, keep themselves far from idolatry and suffer material poverty and whatever else comes their way rather than compromise. All of this comes back to mission. In a very real way, the Church faced a decision between money and mission. They had to choose between godly living and getting along in the financial world.

How could Christians preach there is no god but one and all others represent the vain creations of ignorant men and at the same time worship the emperor? How does the message of taking up one's cross and following Jesus find a hearing when its preachers flee from suffering and worship false gods just to make a fast buck? How can the lost hear the message of an otherworldly kingdom with its own financial and social values when the preachers concern themselves so much with maintaining their success in this world that they will gladly compromise anything and everything?

Clearly, Revelation presupposes the Church cannot be missional and idolatrous at the same time. For many in first-century Asia Minor, mission would cost them their money and financial stability. However, this uncompromising commitment to mission would also affect where they lived. One of Domitian's punishments for refusal to worship him took the form of exile.

Imagine being born in Sardis. Your aunts, uncles, cousins, grandparents, and parents all live on the same street as you. As you walk through the city, you can point out the tree you fell from as a child and skinned your knees. The streets may be dusty and dirty, but they belong to you and your family. Generations of your kith and kin have lived, worked, loved, and died in this place you wouldn't trade for any other. It hasn't been easy, but when the choice came between your business and your faith, you heroically said, "If God can take care of the birds of the air and the flowers of the field, He will meet our needs." When your neighbors shunned you, called you a scab, a coward, un-Roman, and a rebel, you bore their insults and took your bruises with love on your lips — proclaiming a gospel of grace with both words and deeds. Now the glowering centurion bellows, "Worship the emperor or we will confiscate your property and send you away from your family to barbarian lands far away from everything and everyone you have ever known!" What will you do? You see, the church in Asia Minor was not only being asked to pay for mission with their money; they were being asked to pay for it with their very homes as they faced exile for the sake of the gospel.

It doesn't take a genius to see the persecution we have been discussing would not have been limited to financial loss and exile. Indeed, the history of the Early Church drips with the blood of martyrs, and the letter of Revelation, more than any other book in our New Testament, invites the Church to count the cost of mission and to pay it, even when it costs everything. Smyrna is encouraged to be faithful to the point of death (Rev. 2:10); the overcoming in Laodicea after the pattern of Jesus' overcoming implies martyrdom (Rev. 3:21); those under the altar have been slain because of their testimony (Rev. 6:9). The voice from heaven describes God's final victory: "They conquered him because of the blood of the Lamb and because of the word of their testimony, and they did not love their lives even in the face of death" (Rev. 12:11).

The mother of harlots, whom most would agree represents Rome and its empire, is described this way by John: "I saw the woman who had become drunk from the blood of the holy ones and from the blood of those who had made testifying about Jesus the very habit of their lives" (Rev. 17:6). In a further revelation about the fall of Rome personified by the prostitute, John hears the words, "And in her the blood of the prophets and holy ones were found and all those who had been slaughtered in her territory" (Rev. 18:24). A few verses later, heaven sings of God's vengeance upon Rome for killing His servants (Rev. 19:2). Throughout Revelation, again and again, Yahweh reminds us that those who stand firm and who remain missional do so at the risk of losing their very lives to a hostile world system diametrically opposed to God and His kingdom.

So, in considering the church that read the letter of Revelation and entering their world—feeling their fears, hopes, and loves, we will perhaps find we cannot easily judge them. After all, how many of us have such an unshakable commitment to the gospel that we would set aside our riches, homes, and lives to see the world know Him? The church in Revelation faced something few living in the Western world today can even begin to comprehend—a crisis in mission of apocalyptic proportions. For they were a church asking themselves, "Will we stay committed to the mission when it will cost us our money, our homes, and our lives?"

Although countless scholars, preachers, simple believers, heretics, and hacks have spilled barrels of ink in attempts to wrest meaning from the pages of the Apocalypse, too many have forgotten the basics of Bible reading. We cannot understand what a text means until we understand what it meant. The key to what Revelation meant has everything to do with this crisis in mission and this critical question that troubled the hearts of the denizens of first-century Asia Minor. Their question cut to the very heart of the Church's identity. Only when we fully appreciate how, when, and why they asked this question will Revelation begin to make sense to us. Indeed, I would suggest nearly everything in this letter, no matter how dark and mysterious, can be explained when we come to terms with the fact that Revelation was written to help the Church answer the question, *"Will we stay committed to the mission when it will cost us our money, our homes, and our lives?"*

Will we stay committed to the mission when it will cost us our money, our homes, and our lives?

Essentially, John's answer follows two lines: (1) Look at what will happen if we don't give up. (2) Look what will happen if we fail. Do the math, Church. Decide for yourselves whether the mission is worth the cost in light of where the God of the universe has pledged to take us.

REVELATION AND ETHICS

BEFORE WE CAN delve into the subject of this study and consider the songs of Revelation 7, we must think about ethics a bit. I know few of my readers will get warm fuzzy feelings at the mention of ethics, nor will they likely experience Holy Ghost tingling sensations up and down their bodies. Nonetheless, ethics must command the attention of anyone who would understand the words of this prophecy. Dear reader, pay attention: *the book of Revelation is primarily ethical.*

Sometimes we understand a concept best by closely considering its opposite. The opposite of an ethical understanding of Revelation would be that propounded by those who draw charts, identify personages, and imagine very specific postapocalyptic scenarios based on the images of Revelation. The popularity of such works testifies to the allure of an approach to Revelation explaining every conceivable detail using the technology, personalities, places, and trappings of our modern world. Advocates of this approach hold Revelation in one hand and the newspaper in the other—finding helicopters in scorpions, dictators in dragons . . . you name it.

Now, don't get me wrong. I am not trying to say what has been foolishly said time and time again: "I have figured it out. I know the meaning of every symbol in the book of Revelation. Let all interpreters give way to me, and my particular genius." I have *not* figured out every twist and turn of this admittedly very difficult book of the Bible. I *am* saying even *if I had* fully and accurately deciphered every symbol in this letter, it would still be possible for me and my readers to miss the point of Revelation entirely.

Many have made it their hobby to figure out the secret and deep things of God by unraveling the mysteries of Revelation, but to what end? The most popular of these theorists gain fame through their flare for drama, creativity, and the almost science-fiction quality of the stories they weave. These creations effectively make Christians insiders with secret knowledge. So armed, such believers know when everything goes to hell in a handbasket, we insiders face no surprises. Or perhaps, depending on their particular tribulation views, the insiders comfort themselves with the belief that if they work really hard at solving the mystery, just maybe, they will be able to determine what actually happens to those poor saps who miss the Rapture.

> *Anyone who claims to have timetables or even the specific nature of key events laid out like directions in Google Maps is simply guessing.*

I do not intend this obvious caricature to denigrate specula-tors. However, I do hope to communicate that the conclusions of such speculation cannot be proven. I will gladly rejoice with my brothers and sisters who have guessed rightly when the eastern sky breaks, and the Lord appears in all His glory. Still, on this side of Christ's return, anyone who claims to have timetables or even the specific nature of key events laid out like directions in Google Maps is simply guessing.

Now, as I've already said, perhaps they will guess rightly; but a nagging question remains. Did Christ give His bride this beau-tiful letter so we could wonder at the diversity and creativity of its interpreters and their complex explanations? I submit God isn't very interested in any of these things. Rather, He has given us Revelation to change the way we live, to alter our behavior and bring it into conformity with His character. In short, reading Revelation should change the way we do absolutely everything we do.

The glimpse Revelation gives into where God is taking all of his-tory was originally meant to encourage the church in Asia Minor to persist in mission even at the cost of their money, homes, and lives. Understanding that God would one day conquer every foe and present His faithful ones as the ultimate victors was meant to drive these ancient believers to forsake all in obeying God's command to evangelize the world. While the details lack clar-ity, the implications lack none. This vision of the future changes everything, not by providing secret knowledge of key events, but by revealing the unalterable course of history culminating in the absolute victory of those who persist in mission and the ultimate ruin of those who give up.

Revelation encourages us to live lives of utter devotion to Christ by following His command to evangelize the world. Beyond the overarching theme of mission, the purpose of the entire Apocalypse has right living at its core. Sometimes Revelation employs the negative threat of judgment to motivate behavior, but more commonly, the promise of victory and deliverance inspires true Christian living. Yet, we will always miss the point when we drift from the practical behavior Revelation inspires and find ourselves in the realm of science-fiction scenarios. Moreover, I would submit that whereas speculation engenders disagreement and argumentation, the ethics of Revelation promote unity of purpose within the body of Christ. I'll leave it to you to decide which God prefers.

A BOLD SONG OF VICTORY

AS THE CHURCHES of Asia Minor read Revelation, they faced a crisis in mission. They were asking themselves: "Will we stay committed to mission when doing so will cost us our money, our homes, and our lives?" Beyond simply becoming aware of the question itself, you have also come to understand that absolutely everything in the book of Revelation has been crafted to help the Church to answer this question with a resounding and unreserved, "YES, WE WILL!"

Keeping this in mind let's explore a key passage—perhaps *the* key passage—of Revelation. Revelation 7:9–12 "A Bold Song of Victory" where the big picture of Revelation is compressed into a single moment of cosmic history.

First let's pause to consider how Revelation 7:9–12 fits into the flow of the book as a whole. Scholars and pundits like to argue endlessly about the proper outline of the letter, and unsurprisingly, these interpreters have made several different proposals depending on their favored methods and assumptions. The proposal I find most convincing sees Revelation as the story of the unfolding of history, told three times. If we accept this view, then each time the story is told it increases in drama, vividness, and intensity.

Revelation 7:7–12 then comes at the climax of the first telling of the story, and the scene depicts the final realization of our destiny as the people of God. Nonetheless, it matters very little whether you, the reader, accept this view, because everyone would agree this passage represents a climactic moment, if not *the* climactic moment, in redemptive history. Plainly, God here permits us to gaze into His eternal purpose, plan, and place for His people. One's preferred outline for Revelation cannot diminish the magnificence of the view.

> *Amazingly, the place to which God has been directing all of history is actually a worship service.*

Amazingly, the place to which God has been directing all of history is actually a worship service. As the tableau of this cosmic concert unfolds, something incomprehensibly bright and shining in the darkness of the universe dulls and diminishes all other images and arrests our attention. God the Father, in all of His glory, splendor, and radiance, sits enthroned in His heavenly throne room. Surrounding Him stands an expansive choir lifting their voices in worship. The present passage records the lyrics of two of the songs they will sing on that day. We know, in these words, we encounter the music of heaven, because the rhyme and meter of the Greek text indicate these words were not intended for the prose of pulpits but for the praise-filled lips of worshipers. I am calling the first song "A Bold Song of Victory" (Rev. 7:9–10) and the second "A Humble Song of Praise" (Rev. 7:11–12). Here we turn our attention to the first of the two:

> *After I saw these things, behold, there was a great crowd that no one was capable of counting from every nation and tribe and people and tongue standing before the throne and before the Lamb, having been clothed with flowing white robes and holding palm branches in their hands. And they keep crying out in a loud voice:*
>
> > *"Salvation be to our God, who sits upon the throne, and to the Lamb!"*

Only the last line contains the actual words of "The Bold Song of Victory." The other words merely set the song within its proper context by describing the choir charged with the task of kicking off the most spectacular concert of all time.

Consider the choir. Notice its makeup. The first detail grabbing our attention is no one is even capable of counting the crowd of singers gathered around the throne of God. This seems plain enough, but this crowd conceals one of the knottiest interpretative debates of the whole book of Revelation under its flowing white robes: namely, who exactly are these singers? Right before this passage, John has been describing the 144,000, made up of 12,000 people chosen from each of the tribes of Israel, and some say these are simply two different ways of talking about the same group of people.

Note, previously John precisely numbered the crowd of people at 144,000 —whereas here, he simply tells us no one could possibly count the multitude. I am firmly convinced this crowd represents the crowd of the redeemed — all who from throughout all of time have called upon the name of the Lord Jesus unto salvation. It is all of those who belong to Him, the ones He calls His own.

Some readers will not find my explanation convincing, and that's all right. In whatever way we sort out the particulars of their identity, two facts dominate and demand explanation. First, this crowd of singers cannot be counted, and second, somehow its members have the right to sing the song of salvation. Therefore, it seems safe to call it the crowd of the redeemed, and this remains true even if some would exclude certain segments of the redeemed from this particular crowd. However, excluding any branch of God's redeemed people from the crowd seems highly questionable to me based on the fact that the text states every nation stands among their ranks.

Beyond the sheer size of the end-of-time choir/crowd, one immediately notices its extraordinary composition. The members come from everywhere. John takes great pains to highlight the diversity of the redeemed. In confronting this passage featuring an ethnic tapestry, the church in first-century Asia Minor would have been attentive to certain truths. As a mostly Gentile church, they would have been quite struck by the pile of near synonyms modified by the expansive "every."

Every nation (*ethnos*) and people (*laos*) find representation in the multitude. Often these terms serve to distinguish God's chosen people of Israel from everyone else, but here a breathtaking picture of the scope of redemption emerges. The Cross respects no borders. Jewish birth is no advantage, nor is Roman citizenship; God has opened redemption wide to all kinds of people. This view of the wide-open spaces of God's saving action finds more support with the addition of every tribe (*phulē*) and tongue (*glōssa*). *Tribe* does not necessarily equate to blood relation; rather, it often refers to a particular population segment. *Tongue* represents a way of talking about the diversity of human languages.

It would have been sufficient for John to simply have written, "from every nation," but like so often occurs in the Apocalypse, the presentation is calculated to be breathtaking. It is not just diversity but diversity to the nth degree multiplied by infinity. It almost feels exaggerated. However, the grandeur would not have been wasted on the Christians of Asia Minor.

Think back to the crisis in mission the first-century church in Asia Minor faced. Recall this church had the unenviable task of deciding whether they would remain committed to mission — that is, to preaching the gospel with their words and with their lives — in the face of losing their money, homes, and lives. For them, the diversity of this crowd/choir says, "Church in Asia Minor, look what happens if you don't give up!" Indeed, if the civic and imperial authorities should carry them into exile, the gospel would penetrate into the entire known world. They would suffer, lose their homes, be separated from friends and family, and never see their homeland again. Yet, because of their suffering, the nations would be gathered around the throne of God at the end of time, singing a bold song of victory to their God.

This cannot be said to be a case of God working in spite of hardship and suffering. This is different. This end-time cosmic choir cannot come about any other way. The choir comes into existence not in spite of suffering but because of it. Exile itself, in God's hands, would be the instrument by which He would bring the gospel to the nations. The church in Asia Minor had to decide whether it would compromise the gospel and avoid the pain of exile or embrace exile and the gospel.

If they could bear it, suffering would become an opportunity to preach the gospel in unreached lands. If the Church stays committed to mission, it will gain the nations. Ultimately, the ethnic diversity of the crowd of the redeemed demonstrates that perseverance in mission actually results in the fulfillment of the Great Commission of Matthew 28:19–20. Go! Teach the nations (*ethnos*)!

Perhaps more startling than the size and diversity of the crowd is its posture. The text reports an unbelievable scene. This mighty throng actually has the audacity to *stand* before the throne of God. If we don't consider this carefully, we may miss the strangeness of such a spectacle.

Throughout the Bible, God conscientiously keeps human beings at a safe distance from His manifest presence. When Moses longs to see the face of God, he has to take the consolation prize of seeing God's back. Furthermore, God informs him that no one can see His face and live (Ex. 33:20–23).

Although there are some exceptions to this in Scripture, usually when just a glimmer of the glory and majesty of God becomes visible, at the very least, no one can stand up. Consider the dedication of Solomon's temple (2 Chron. 5:14); when the glory of the Lord filled the temple, the priests couldn't even stand. Or think about Ezekiel's commission; he saw a powerful vision of the glory and majesty of God, and he fell on his face (Ezek. 1:28). However, if we think about this image from the perspective of the New Testament, we might find it less shocking. After all, many people did see Jesus, whom we know to have been God in the flesh. Additionally, at the coming transition of the ages portrayed in Revelation 7, we confidently expect that the full knowledge anticipated in 1 Corinthians 13 will become a reality. That day, all Christians will indeed see God face to face and know Him just as they are known by Him.

Nonetheless, in light of everything we know of the manifest presence of God the Father, it seems supremely odd this enumerable crowd of the redeemed would have the unmitigated gall to stand nonchalantly in the glory and radiance of God the Father in His heavenly throne room. Is it just me, or is this really, really, weird? Notice too we are not talking about a gathering of the Pauls and Peters of the Kingdom. This is not just the really "good" people; it is absolutely everyone who calls Him Lord. The whole picture makes me think two things: (1) Wow, what boldness! (2) How did that happen?

The boldness probably should not surprise me, or anyone for that matter, considering what the crowd/choir is wearing. John reports they have been dressed in flowing white robes. One point English readers may miss here concerns the divine passive mood of the Greek perfect participle. Don't worry about the grammatical mumbo jumbo. The sense is quite simple. The choir hasn't gone to some celestial closet and picked out flowing white robes for themselves. God himself dressed them, and He selected this particular garment to pay them a high honor—one only God himself can grant.

The wardrobe takes us back to the church in Sardis in Revelation 3. Here God promises the victorious they will be clothed in white garments. (Again, the divine passive is used.) As we discussed earlier, being victorious or overcoming has to do with continuing to live missional lives in spite of pressure to abandon missionary living. Those who make it to the end, those who make up the crowd/choir of the redeemed, are the very ones who refused to abandon their devotion to preaching the gospel with words and deeds even at the cost of their money, their homes, and their lives.

It does not take much imagination to understand such people might have some boldness. The robes do not produce boldness; rather, they reflect it. The true source of boldness lies in what the people hold in their hands: the palm branches. By the way, you may notice a nagging corollary to this scene: the harsh reality that those who choose money, home, and life over mission do not receive white robes and do not join the crowd of the redeemed. If this offends, I can only say the author of Revelation simply can't imagine an authentic Christian who lacks what many today would call the missionary zeal of an extremist.

As I have just intimated, the palm branches hold the answer to the question, "How did that happen?" The palm branch carries a threefold significance. First, it makes one think of the Feast of Succoth, or what you probably have heard called the Feast of Tabernacles. During the feast, Jews traditionally built tent-like shelters, which they covered with palm branches. This feast commemorates the wilderness wanderings of the people of Israel and God's provision for His people during those years. However, it has a further significance in that it also functions as a military memorial, which calls attention to the role of God in leading His people to military victory over the peoples who had inhabited the Promised Land.

In the Roman world, the palm branch carried a similar meaning. When a Roman general returned from the battlefield in victory, magnificent parades ensued with people holding palm branches as a symbol of victory. Just such a parade happened when Tiberius destroyed the temple in Jerusalem in AD 70 and returned to Rome with its sacred vessels as war trophies. The palm branch as a symbol of victory also held a prominent place in athletic events in the Greco-Roman tradition. Often, those who won an event at the games, whether in Corinth, Thessaly, or Olympia, were presented with palm branches as a symbol of their victory in competition.

The palm branch also makes us think of the triumphal entry when Jesus entered into Jerusalem riding on a donkey. On this occasion, the crowds cut down palm branches and threw them before Jesus—paving His entry into Jerusalem (Matt. 21:5–9; Mark 11:8–11; John 12:12–15). Interestingly, only John, who very possibly wrote both the Gospel of John and the book of Revelation, makes a point of telling us in his gospel that the branches were *palm* branches. The significance of the palm branch has obvious implications for readers attuned to the image.

The people of Jerusalem on this day greeted Jesus as a general, and they decided to have a victory parade by faith. They expressed their belief in Jesus as the one who would launch a holy war against Rome and restore the throne of David to its power and glory. As it turned out, Jesus had a different path to victory in mind, and it would not lead to a battlefield with legions arrayed against holy warriors but to a skull-shaped hill where He would suffer the scandalous and humiliating death of a failed revolutionary.

Indeed, when the crowds of Jerusalem realized Jesus had a different sort of victory in mind, they themselves replaced their "Hosanna!" with "Crucify him!" I would contend only in Revelation 7 do we finally see the full scope of the true victory Jesus had in mind that day. He did not rebuke the crowds and say, "No, no, you have it all wrong. I did not come to defeat evil empires and oppressors. I have simply come to teach you to love." He accepted their victory parade, and He did win a victory. However, this victory is so large, so cosmic in nature one can only see it by zooming the lens of perception out until all of human history can be seen at once. Although different parts of the New Testament hint at the scope and grandeur of Christ's triumph, only the wide-angle lens of the Apocalypse puts it fully into its proper perspective.

Unmistakably, the palm branches in the hands of the crowd/ choir powerfully testify to a victory, but the centrality of this victory only becomes fully apparent as we listen to the words of the song on their lips: *"Salvation be to our God, who sits upon the throne, and to the Lamb!"*

The first word of the song, "salvation," *soteria* in Greek, focuses the whole course of cosmic history to the finest point of a pin. *Soteria* signifies not simply a spiritual experience, but rather, it speaks of an oppressed, tormented, and frightened people being delivered from sure destruction by means of military rescue. Here history is reduced to a victory brought about by the plan of God the Father; for salvation is to Him who sits on the throne. The victory equally belongs to God's agent of victory, namely, His Son Jesus; for salvation is also to the Lamb. Only here do we finally grasp the full breadth of the triumph of the triumphal entry.

As the church in Asia Minor took in the sights and sounds of the final worship service, they noticed the choir standing, clothed in white, holding palm branches, and singing the Bold Song of Victory. They would have heard the still, clear voice of their Father whispering a message of encouragement in their ears. "It is true if you persist in mission, if you don't give up and you don't give in, you may lose your money, your homes, and your lives. Still, know this, a day is coming when every force opposing my gospel will be brought low. I will defeat them all, and they will be swallowed up in victory. That day, no town councilman who would ruin your business, no centurion who would carry you into exile, no tribune who would torture or crucify or behead you will be able to stand. Not even the military might of Rome will hold any sway. Church, no matter what they do to you, there is a day coming when it is you who will be holding the palm branch of victory firmly in your hand; it will most certainly not be your enemies."

It would be a mistake to mute in any way the clearly militaristic implications found in such a vivid portrayal of victory. The church in Asia Minor, struggling with its commitment to mission, was not facing a purely spiritual enemy. Their enemy had real power to break bones and to draw blood. Their enemy had the power to take food from the mouths of their children. Their enemy had the wherewithal to banish them from loved ones. The message of Revelation doesn't pretend our flesh-and-blood enemies can be taken away by simply spiritualizing them, nor does it promise bliss in place of hardship. It does, however, promise history is headed to a place of victory, and no matter how strong our foes may be, no matter what they take, and no matter what we, the Church, might suffer, in the end, *we win!*

The victory Jesus won on the cross means the powers of the world opposed to the gospel will, with absolute certainty, reach a day when God will utterly crush them—leaving them vanquished and impotent. The Church, the people of God, will hold the palm branches that day.

THE SOUNDTRACK OF YOUR LIFE

NOW THAT WE have looked at the Bold Song of Victory, I want to pause for a minute to consider the implications of this song for everyday life. Again, let me emphasize something I mentioned previously. Many people hold the wrong idea about Revelation. They regard this book like abstract art. It's interesting to look at once in a while. It's mildly entertaining to guess at the meaning of the unearthly shapes described on its pages, but the strange images fail to connect to life in the *real* world. Nothing could be further from the truth!

Revelation is the most practical book in the New Testament. Every word, every image, every symbol asks the reader to change his or her life. This book demands very specific action from us. The universe-enveloping image of triumph contained in the music of this Bold Song of Victory in many ways focuses Revelation's many pleas for action into a single, crystal-clear summon. This song demands all who hear it conform their thinking, attitudes, and actions to fit the kind of life Jesus calls us to—a missional life. In other words, the words, notes, and melody of the song comprise the ever-present soundtrack of the Christian life.

Revelation is the most practical book in the New Testament.

If you have ever watched a movie, you know just how important the music is. I love *Star Wars*, and when I watched the special features for episode 4, I learned George Lucas almost used some weird 1970s disco music to score the first movie. Watching some of my favorite scenes with the wrong music would change the entire feeling and meaning of the story. Without John Williams's "Dun Dun Dun Dadadun Dadadun," Darth Vader would be just some freakishly tall guy in a bad cape. With the music, Vader becomes a menacing bad guy. The audience knows how to feel about him. They know he is the enemy of all that is good. I apologize if *Star Wars* isn't your thing.

The point is in stories told through film or even in live musicals and operas, the music puts the actions of the characters into context. The music tells us how to feel about them. The music cues us to the significance of the events we are witnessing. Wouldn't it be nice if life were like the movies? Wouldn't it be nice if life came with a soundtrack to put everything into context, to reveal the true nature of the events we are living through, and to help us anticipate what comes next in the story? Well, it turns out in Revelation, God gave us just such a soundtrack. Just like a movie, where the audience needs the music most at moments of great uncertainty in order to grasp the story, Revelation's soundtrack is most necessary in moments of difficulty and doubt. In the story of God's church in America, I think we desperately need a really good soundtrack.

For the church in Asia Minor in the first-century, the Bold Song of Victory put an image of the future into their heads. This image of the future served to reframe their understanding of the present. They weren't expected to listen to the song just one time. John expected them to replace whatever soundtrack played in the background of their lives with this new soundtrack. They needed to process their crisis in mission through this music. As I explained in the last chapter, the music of victory moved them to decide whether they would be willing to pay the high cost of faithfulness in mission. Would they preach the gospel and order their entire lives around fulfilling the Great Commission when doing so would cost them their money, their homes, and maybe even their lives?

Now, understand our spiritual ancestors didn't answer this question in one decisive moment. They gave their answer moment by moment as they lived their daily lives. At the market buying food, a woman from Ephesus faced a decision. Will I tell this bread merchant about Jesus? Will I risk my home so he can hear the gospel? At these moments, you can almost hear the song of victory in the background increasing in volume. It shouts, "Consider the future! Consider the crowd gathered around the throne! Yes, there is risk. Yes, this small choice may have a high cost. However, make your decision based on the future, not on your fear!"

It's in just these moments of everyday decisions in life, where the rubber meets the road, that Revelation fulfills its purpose. Its music forming the soundtrack of our lives constantly draws our decision-making activity away from our present fears and into the future. It reminds us we do not belong to this uncertain and dangerous world, but to another world from which all uncertainty and all possibility of loss and defeat have been banished. At the end of the day, the future isn't a matter of speculation and guessing. The future, presented in Revelation, gives us Christians the practical tools we need in order to make every decision of our lives in light of the mission God gave us to proclaim salvation to the world.

I can't repeat it enough—Revelation from beginning to end concerns mission. Jesus commanded us to go and preach in Matthew 28:19–20, but Revelation unpacks what a life of obedience to His commission really looks like. As the Bold Song of Victory teaches us, true obedience doesn't count any present cost too high for the future reward of the nations gathered around the throne of God in victorious worship. The salvation of our neighbors and those on the other side of the globe who have yet to hear is worth our money, our homes, and our lives. However, it would be a mistake to think Revelation's call to mission was on the level of pulling nominal Christians from lukewarm mediocrity into dynamic missional living. What we have been talking about isn't a matter of changing the soundtrack of our lives from decently acceptable music to truly awesome and inspiring music.

At this point, I must remind you Revelation is an apocalypse. This means it isn't a book about getting along in the world by finding a comfortable gray zone in which to live life safely under the radar. Apocalyptic literature views the world in stark contrasts. From this perspective, this book reveals the world and its system possess no redeeming qualities. They are wholly evil . . . destined for destruction and judgment. In contrast, God and His kingdom contain no trace of evil or darkness in them, and those who choose to live under His rule dare not compromise with the world in any way, shape, or form.

This takes us back to the seven churches. Revelation makes us aware of three responses as they faced their crisis in mission.

Some denounced mission and simply embraced the values and practices of Rome because they judged the cost of missional living too high. Others took a middle path. They domesticated mission—fusing Greco-Roman idolatry and immorality with Christianity. Without going so far as to embrace idolatry, others on this middle way simply became zombie Christians. They strove to live as Christians but abandoned the riskiest part of relationship with Christ, i.e., they stopped proclaiming the good news. Still others threw all caution to the wind and remained faithful even to the point of death. In short, faced with the question "Will we stay committed to mission when it will cost us our money, our homes, and our lives?" these radicals answered, "Yes!"

Because in this book, we focus on the two songs of Revelation 7, we approach the missions message of Revelation mostly from a positive angle. The vision of the future inspires missional living now. However, it would be irresponsible to ignore the fact that Revelation puts much weight on the negative side of things. Indeed, as we noted, the churches in Asia Minor responded to their crisis of mission in three ways: (1) denouncing mission, (2) domesticating mission, and (3) doubling down on mission. However, Revelation only endorses one of the three responses. Of course, I am speaking of the all-in response of those who doubled down on mission to the point of being willing to give everything to see the gospel of the kingdom advance.

We must ask. What of those who abandoned their commission? What of those who domesticated the gospel in order to escape suffering on account of Christ? For them, Revelation unveils dire consequences.

In Ephesus, we learn those who fail in mission will have their lampstand removed (Rev. 2:5); but on the flip side, those in Ephesus who persist in mission will get to eat from the tree of life. The unspoken yet clear implication is those who fail to persist in mission will not taste the fruit of the tree of life. In Smyrna, those who remain faithful to the point of death receive the promise of the crown of life and immunity from the power of the second death. Again, the reverse implication cannot escape notice. Those who fail in mission will surely not escape the second death (Rev. 2:10–11).

Pergamum and Thyatira provide examples of compromise. These churches tried to stay safe by domesticating the gospel and blending it with pagan practice. However, they are called to repent lest God himself make war against them and lest they receive His judgment for their deeds (Rev. 2:14–16, 23). God also calls Sardis to return to their former gospel-proclaiming lifestyle. If they fail to do so, God himself will come against them as a thief in the night, and it is implied their names will be removed from the Book of Life (Rev. 2:3–5). The letters to the churches unlock the mysteries of Revelation, and their clear connection of judgment with missional failure and compromise suggests the tragedy of failure in mission touches on every scene of judgment in the book of Revelation, including chapter 21's terrible lake of fire.

We cannot forget that beyond its reassuring promises of victory for those who remain faithful in the mission of the Church, Revelation also includes frightening promises of judgment for those who fail. Those who denounce and those who domesticate mission make themselves God's enemies. They become those against whom the armies of heaven will fight. They become the enemies of the Lamb, and they will not escape His wrath. Nothing will shield them from the sharp sword coming from His mouth.

Just as the images of victory encourage the Church, and especially individual Christians, to make every decision in light of the future rather than present fears, so the images of judgment remind us mission is no light matter. Missions is not an add-on to Christianity. It isn't a special activity for supersaints. The missional life is the Christian life. If we abandon our mission and commission for the sake of protecting our money, homes, and lives, we in fact abandon Christ. We transition from being God's friends to being His enemies.

Revelation doesn't just inspire missional living; it also warns against missional treason. Again, let me remind you, the enterprise of mission is an apocalyptic enterprise. It offers no comfortable, gray path. The mission of the Church is clearly delineated. From the perspective of Revelation, our attitude toward mission marks us. Are we all in, or all out? There is no middle way, and therefore, if we fail in missions, we fail in everything.

This may sound harsh. However, remember John penned Revelation for those experiencing hard times. When everything in life gets difficult, we need a means of separating the essential from the nonessential. When missions begins to cost too much, the Church naturally wonders about it. Does our mission really belong in the category of "essential"? Or does mission better fit in the category of "nonessential"?

The positive image of the salvation of the nations and absolute victory coupled with the negative warnings of judgment work together to erase all ambiguity. No one who takes Revelation seriously questions the place of missions in the Christian life. Our mission to take the gospel to the world occupies an absolutely central place in the Christian life. So much so, if we abandon mission, we abandon not just the present Christian life but also the life to come.

I don't apologize for this statement, but it isn't what I'm driving at. Listen, being apocalyptically missional people affects everyday life. In other words, every Christian needs to make the Bold

Song of Victory the soundtrack of his or her life. When this happens, our every decision will derive from the future God revealed rather than from whatever fears and uncertainties characterize our present circumstances.

It occurs to me some may be skeptical about basing our entire lives on a few verses from arguably the strangest book of the Bible. However, this notion of looking to the future as the authoritative guide to determine our actions in the present isn't unique to the book of Revelation. In fact, the idea for Christians that the future controls the present is one of the most pervasive ideas in the New Testament. In theological terms, we call this concept *inaugurated eschatology*. Don't panic! It sounds complicated, but it is really very simple. It means through the work and life of Jesus, the world changed forever.

The world changed because the rule and reign of God known as the kingdom of God invaded the world through Jesus Christ. This means God's kingdom has *already* become a present reality. However, God, and with Him, His kingdom, has *not yet* conquered the world. God's rule and reign is both present and future. Let me anchor this thought in Scripture for you.

Jesus himself, through His beatitudes, taught us to think in terms of the *already* and *not yet*. Just consider the Beatitudes from the Sermon on the Mount, and as you do, pay close attention to the present and future tenses of the italicized verbs.

> The poor in spirit are blessed because the kingdom of the heavens *is* theirs.

> Those who mourn are blessed because they *will be* comforted.

> The gentle are blessed because they *will inherit* the earth.

Those who hunger and thirst for righteousness are blessed because they *will be* satisfied.

The merciful are blessed because they *will be* shown mercy.

Those who are pure in heart are blessed because they *will see* God.

Those who make peace are blessed because they *will be* called sons of God.

Those who have been persecuted on account of righteousness are blessed because the kingdom of the heaven *is* theirs.

You *are* blessed whenever they *revile* you, *persecute* you, and falsely *say* all sorts of evil things against you on account of me. *Rejoice* and *be glad* because your reward will be great in heaven. For, in this way, they *persecuted* the prophets who were before you.

Here, in the Beatitudes, Jesus introduces the nature of God's kingdom. Remember Matthew often uses "kingdom of heaven," while Luke and Paul prefer "kingdom of God." Don't be distracted by this. Though the expressions differ, the meaning remains the same, namely, God's rule and reign. Notice the first beatitude and the last two beatitudes are in the present tense.[1] They declare the present blessedness of those who heard Jesus' words. In meeting Jesus and hearing His sermon, those people had *already* begun to experience the rule and reign of God.

---

1. I have italicized all of the verbs that appear in the Greek text. However, I have had to supply some verbs that weren't in the original in order to make the English readable.

Later in Matthew's gospel, when the crowds saw Jesus cast out demons, they had, in doing so, experienced the supernatural and cosmic power of the Holy Spirit associated with God's reign. For this reason, Jesus says, "But if I cast out demons by the Spirit of God, then the kingdom of God has come upon you" (Matt. 12:28). This is important: the supernatural power of the Holy Spirit visible in healings, exorcisms, and all of the gifts of the Spirit proves God's kingdom has broken into the world and is *already* a present reality. However, when Jesus spoke the six middle beatitudes, He used the future tense. As much as the life-changing power of the kingdom of God can be tasted and experienced by those who follow Jesus, it also remains incomplete. It waits for future consummation.

Significantly, the entire Sermon on the Mount introduces the concept of the kingdom of God in order to teach ethics. The present and future nature of God's reign undergirds the Christian life. It tells us what to do with our money. It instructs us how to interact with the government. It gives us instructions on forgiveness, on prayer, on every aspect of living in the world. Because of this, it is no surprise the Sermon on the Mount became the new believer's class for the Early Church.

New Testament writers such as Paul and James based their ethical instructions upon the principles found in that sermon. The first-century Christian discipleship document known as the *Didache* does the same thing. It's not too much to say that the entire ethical worldview of the first Christians derives from Jesus' words as He preached on the mountain. In other words, in good times and bad, when it's hard to obey and when it's easy, in wealth and in poverty, in the East and in the West, in every conceivable circumstance of life, the principles of Sermon on the Mount ought to guide the concrete, practical actions of everyday Christians.

Now, this guidance consists of more than just "turning the other cheek." The genius of the Sermon on the Mount goes deeper than the specific commands Jesus issued in it. The sermon actually redefines reality. It lets us know in no uncertain terms we Christians may live in the world like everyone else, but not in the same way. Why?

We live differently in the world because we know something those outside of the Church do not. We know presidents, kings, congresses, parliaments, and even nations do not have the real power. In fact, we know their time is coming to an end, because we have met and have become friends with the soon coming King. He has already invaded the world, but only we insiders know about the invasion. Only we have tasted and seen a power and authority that makes all human governments and rulers seem like kids playing at leadership. More than that, King Jesus has let us in on His plan.

He intends slowly and steadily to draw more and more of the world into His rule until one day, His rule–His kingdom–will eclipse every human ruler, authority, and power. Paul describes that day in Philippians 2:10 when he says, "so that at the name of Jesus every knee of those in heaven, and of those upon the earth, and of those under the earth might bow and every tongue might confess that Jesus

> *One day all the future tenses of the Beatitudes will become present experiences. Until that day, we live between the times.*

Christ is Lord to the glory of God the Father." It just so happens this is the same day our passage in Revelation 7 has in mind as well.

One day all the future tenses of the Beatitudes will become present experiences. Until that day, we live between the times. We live in a world into which the Kingdom has *already* come. We also wait for the day when the undeniable reality and power of God's kingdom will come in fullness. We long for a time when the world with its evils, cruelties, racism, injustices, and even viruses will be set right by the reality of the fully present and universal reign of God.

> **In the meantime, we live in the present by the rules of the future.**

But what do we do in the meantime? In the meantime, we live in the present by the rules of the future. This is in essence what the Sermon on the Mount is all about. In it, Jesus teaches us what it means to live in this world without living by its rules and values. Christians don't fear what regular people fear. We don't anxiously ask, "What will I eat?" We aren't obsessed with what we will wear or where we will live. Instead, we trust the King to provide for His subjects. We don't pursue our own honor. We don't demand our own rights. We don't deprive others of their rights or dignity. We don't hold grudges. The list goes on.

This is what Paul means when he says, "For your citizenship is in the heavens" (Phil. 3:20). Indeed, as Paul corrects the behavior of his fledgling churches, this otherworldly way of living in the present by the rules of the future always lies near the surface of his thought. In short, Paul urges his churches to stop playing by the rules of the world. He begs them to stop counting success the way the world does. He implores his congregations to live by the rules of the future and sever all ties with this present world's way of doing things.

You may be wondering at this point if I have lost sight of Revelation. I haven't. Here's the connection. The idea of our every action as Christians being shaped by a vision of the future *is not* unique to the Apocalypse. Thanks to Jesus, the entire New

Testament conceptualizes Christian ethics in this way. We, as Christians, absolutely and unequivocally believe in the future, God's kingdom will arrive in force. When it does, all human governments, rulers, and societies will come to nothing.

We, as believers, *already* live under the rule of the coming Kingdom and also *already* taste its power. Thus, we choose to make our decisions and live our lives—in a practical, not just a spiritual sense—by the rules, values, and demands of the Kingdom. We live in the present by the rules of the future. This isn't just Revelation. This is the New Testament and the entire Christian life.

However, there is something unique about Revelation. In the case of Revelation, the rules of the future are applied with great detail, care, and precision to the subject of missions. As we have seen, when we live by the rules of the future in a missional sense, we willingly give up our money, our homes, and our lives so the world may know Him . . . so the nations will experience the joy and rapture of being subjects of the King of kings and Lord of lords.

Having come this far, I hope you see how practical Revelation is. I also hope you have begun to long for the Bold Song of Victory to become the soundtrack of your life. What would that look like during a pandemic like the one we are experiencing? In the face of questions like this, the blessing of a Pentecostal heritage really comes in handy. For generations now, without talking about it in quite this way, we in the Assemblies of God engaged in missions apocalyptically. The pages of our history are replete with those who have been willing to lay aside their money, homes, and lives in order to do their part in fulfilling the Great Commission. This was especially the case when our spiritual forefathers and foremothers faced the great flu pandemic of 1918.

In April 1914, the Assemblies of God held its first General Council in Hot Springs, Arkansas. In November the same year in Chicago, the Council approved a resolution summarizing the Assembly of God's raison d'être: "We commit ourselves and the movement to Him for the greatest evangelism that the world has ever seen. We pledge our hearty co-operation, prayers and help to this end."[2] Many who read this know these basic facts, but did you ever stop to consider the timing of our birth as a missions movement? Three months after the meeting in Hot Springs, the first shots of World War I rang out. A few years later, American soldiers joined the conflict. The war to end all wars was certainly not the setting anyone would have chosen under which to launch the boldest, most comprehensive evangelism effort in the history of the world. To top it all off, when the war ended and the troops started returning home, they brought the Spanish flu virus with them.

By October 1918, the *Christian Evangel* was reporting fifteen to eighteen people were dying each day in Springfield, Missouri.[3] They had their own lockdown experience, in which they were unable to go to work or to church. Interestingly, they processed these experiences apocalyptically. The flu and the massive upheavals in the world convinced them the end-time events were unfolding before their eyes; they believed the worst was yet to come, and they believed little time remained before the coming of the Lord. At the same time, these early Pentecostals emphasized God's people need not fear.[4] In place of fear, recognizing the apocalyptic nature of their times and perceiving a spiritual battle underway around them, they sprang into action. In particular, they organized prayer conventions in response to their pandemic.

---

2. *Combined Minutes of the General Council of the Assemblies of God in the United States of America, Canada and Foreign Lands* (Gospel Publishing House, St. Louis, 1914), 12.
3. *The Christian Evangel*, May 3 (1919), 3.
4. "The Spanish Influenza" in *The Christian Evangel*, October 19 (1918), 4.

In 1919, all over the world, Pentecostal believers gathered for prayer in what they called "prayer conventions," and they were not just praying for healing. Their real concern lay in something deeper and more significant than their own health, comfort, safety, and well-being. One of the organizers of the prayer convention movement, Thomas Myerscough, brings home the exigencies of his day and the impetus of the prayer conventions with these moving words:

> Truly we need to exercise faith for the manifestation of much more *of* God's presence and power to counteract the furious onslaughts of the devil. In less than twelve month's time, Spanish influenza has caused the death of human beings, in multitudes, simultaneously, in all quarters of the globe. In India alone, literally millions have succumbed to this deadly pestilence. Since the demon powers have been permitted to create destruction of human life by millions and on a world wide scale, is it not reasonable that believers should exercise faith for the redemption of millions of souls to be accomplished in a short time and throughout the length and breadth of the world? Surely God's resources are greater than the devil's.[5]

Notice where all the weight of their energy and concern falls squarely on the "redemption of millions of souls"—the never reached.

As these believers rushed to organize their prayer conventions, they issued guidelines for prayer. At the conventions, they would not flock around well-known speakers, nor would they seek personal spiritual experiences. Rather, they would give most of their

---

5. "Prayer Conventions," in *The Christian Evangel*, May 3 (1919), 3.

time to "united and importunate intercession for the main thing in view, namely, a fresh and mighty outpouring of the Holy Ghost."[6] Why pray for a fresh outpouring of the Spirit? Their answer can be summed up in one word—dissatisfaction.

> While we praise God with thanksgiving that the Latter Rain has been falling in recent years and Pentecost has in a very real sense has come according to Acts 2:4, it is our deep conviction that the Pentecostal Movement *has not measured up* to the degree of apostolic power recorded in the Book of Acts, for in the apostolic times God's power was manifested in salvation of sinners in great multitudes.[7]

These pioneers of modern Pentecost were dissatisfied with the extent to which the lost were being reached. How could they be satisfied when the never reached remained untouched and in danger? The pandemic raised this dissatisfaction to a fever pitch, so they dropped everything; they threw caution and safety to the wind, and they gathered en masse to pray. Being convinced the end was near, viewing the world apocalyptically, they focused all of their attention on the task of the Great Commission.

In a sense, this early generation of Pentecostal saints faced the same crisis in mission the first-century churches in Asia Minor faced. Gripped by a deadly pandemic, would they remain committed to mission when doing so would cost them their money, their homes, and their lives? Their prayer proves they understood the importance of this question and they knew they could only answer yes with the supernatural help of the Holy Spirit. But how did they respond to their crisis in mission? What was their answer?

---

6. Ibid.
7. Ibid. Emphasis mine.

When it comes to money, the answer is clear. In 1916, the Assemblies of God gave $4,879.50 to world missions. They gave $10,223.98 in 1917, and in 1918, they nearly tripled their giving to $29,630.51. Amid 1919's deadly third wave of the pandemic, they further increased their missions giving to $63,548.59.[8] As in 2020, at different points in that earlier period, mines, restaurants, factories, and churches were closed and quarantines imposed. Moreover, the Spanish flu hit males between the ages of eighteen and forty the hardest, so many families lost their primary breadwinner.

In this context, the Assemblies of God, as a movement gave sacrificially. They gave more, not less. They did this because they believed time was short. They anticipated Jesus' return at any moment. Most importantly, they believed the solemn task of carrying the gospel to the never reached was worth their money, even in a moment of financial scarcity. Our forefathers and mothers did all of this so missionaries might carry the marvelous gospel of Christ to the never reached.

They also went. Between 1918 and 1919, the number of Assemblies of God world missionaries increased from 120 to 195. At a time when authorities told people to stay home . . . at a time when professionals warned people about the world being a dangerous place, our spiritual grandparents and great-grandparents went. They willingly left their homes so others might know Jesus. It wasn't safe for them to go, and it wasn't safe for them to stay on the mission field either. In those pandemic years, obituaries of missionaries who stayed at their posts in spite of great danger and hardship peppered the pages of the *Christian Evangel*. For instance, in these pandemic years, missionaries continued

8. "Missionary Treasurer's Report," in *The Christian Evangel*, October 18 (1919), 2.

to serve in Liberia, living in houses with mud floors and leaky roofs. According to the General Council's report, "In consequence of these unhealthy conditions many of our missionaries have become very sick and some died."[9]

No doubt remains; faced with their own pandemic, not dissimilar to ours, the first members of this great missions movement we call the Assemblies of God viewed the world in an apocalyptic way. They allowed the vision of the future, the vision of the nations gathered around the throne of God at the end of time, to determine their actions. They did not live by fear but by the future. Therefore, they willingly laid down their money, their homes, and their lives in order to fulfill the Great Commission of the Master.

The pressures that tempt us to abandon our mission remain fairly constant. The ancient Church faced them, the early Pentecostals faced them, and even missionaries who go to the field during the best of times face them. Let me assure you as career missionaries, my family and I faced them many times during the last fifteen years. In the midst of our first term in the Philippines, at different points, we definitely asked ourselves, "Is mission worth our money, our home, and our lives?"

No one will marvel to learn that being a missionary does not bring lucrative financial benefits. Between my wife and I, we hold five college degrees. Before going into missions, we both received good job offers promising to provide a much more comfortable life than the one we experience in missions. We have never regretted our decision to obey God's call to live the life of missionaries. We find God always takes care of our needs. Still, there have certainly been moments when I have been very cognizant our choice has meant having less than we might otherwise have.

---

9. Ibid.

American culture, in ways both subtle and obvious, tells us to strive for possessions and comfort and to measure our worth by comparing ourselves with others. Are the never reached worth our money? Almost everyone reading this book has made sacrifices for the sake of missions. Some of you have sacrificed more than my family. Yet, we never get beyond the point of asking this all-important question, especially when times get hard and our savings dwindle: Is the mission worth our money? If we do not remain vigilant, the allure of worldly security easily extinguishes missionary passion.

The pressures of the mission field extend far beyond finances. When we boarded the plane for a three-year term in the Philippines, we took with us my wife's parents' only three grandchildren. At the time, our kids were six weeks, two years, and four years of age. Moreover, my mother-in-law has been paralyzed from the waist down since the age of fourteen. It would be quite impossible for her to make the twenty-plus-hour trip sitting up in planes and airports. Nor could we afford a midterm visit home. For all intents and purposes, our mission would cost us our home—not just the streets and the sense of belonging associated with a beloved hometown but in personal connection with loved ones. Every missionary, from time to time, finds himself or herself asking: Is missions worth my home?

More than the emotional pain of separation from friends and family and the forsaking of comfort, we, along with many engaged in full-time missionary work, sometimes find our lives at risk. Riots, coup attempts, bombings, kidnappings, and guerrilla groups formed the background noise of our life in the Philippines. Personally, we never directly experienced any of these dangers. Our area remained fairly secure and untouched by these kinds of calamities and threats. Still, on occasion, the danger of death invaded our otherwise placid lives.

I remember one occasion in particular. My wife suddenly collapsed to the floor of our house with severe chest pains. She struggled to breath and experienced difficulty remaining conscious. There was no 911 to call, no ambulance with trained paramedics available. I put her in the car and rushed her down a switchback mountain road to the hospital. All along the way, I kept praying, but also thinking to myself, "How am I going to raise three kids by myself?" Every once in a while, I would ask her if she was okay. Sometimes she responded; sometimes she didn't. On that occasion, a gall-bladder attack caused the problem, and we traveled to Manila for surgery.

A few months later, we repeated the same drama. This time, however, she suffered acute appendicitis. When we arrived at our local mountain hospital, the doctors said, "There is no time to take her to Manila. She could die on the way. We have to operate." This hospital lacked soap in the emergency room for patients or doctors. Dirty sheets covered the beds. People walked in and out of the operating room freely. Just outside the operating room open windows allowed drafts of outside air into the hallway. People came and went without washing or putting on masks. Ants crawled up and down the IV in Lindsey's arm. Very few Westerners would be happy to be receiving treatment at such a facility. But what could we do? It was either drive to Manila to the good hospital and risk death on the way or stay in the mountains and risk death. Either way, I faced the distinct possibility of being a single parent.

We chose an operation in the mountains. The attendants took my wife in for a simple operation which took nearly five hours. As the minutes ticked by, I kept reading the Psalms and tried not to worry that the simple surgery continued so long. When the doctor finally came to talk to me, she said, "We're just lucky a cardiologist happened to be here. Your wife had a serious heart problem during the operation, and had the cardiologist not been here to administer a life-saving drug at just the right moment, she would have surely had a stroke or died on the table."

In the months following, my wife faced more problems with her heart, and eventually, a doctor in Thailand told us she could drop dead at any moment. His prescription made her so tired she could barely move. This medication produced some even more serious side effects, one of which was a feeling like her heart was vibrating in her chest. Neither of us could sleep at night, because we both feared she might not wake up. Eventually, we decided to return to the United States for a medical furlough to get to the bottom of the heart issue.

On our way out, the Lord orchestrated the timing so that we caught a flight between two typhoons that ravaged the Philippines. Any small change in our plans and my wife would have developed a potentially fatal reaction to the medication right as the second typhoon hit the Philippines. As it was, she had this reaction in the States, where it was taken care of quickly. Had we stayed, we would have been desperate to get her to Manila in the middle of the second typhoon, which washed out the road we would have traveled and killed two hundred people in the area where we lived. My entire family and I would have almost certainly died. To this tale, I could add the agony of having our one-year-old son tested for the potentially fatal dengue fever and praying while we awaited the test results. We also faced more mundane challenges such as culture shock—a trial no one except those who have spent more than a year immersed in another culture can fully understand.

What is the point of rehearsing the hardships of the mission field to you? Most certainly, it is not an attempt to make you view me or my family as heroes, or any nonsense of the sort. Indeed, of all the missionaries I know personally, you should probably consider us among the wimpiest out there. Others have faced far more, suffered far more, and lost far more than we have. Our little story gives you a picture of the absolute least which will happen to the person or family that commits wholeheartedly to mission. The point I am driving at is there were lots of days when my family and I felt like giving up. There were days when we asked, "Is the mission worth this? Is it worth our money, our home, and our lives?" Everyone who dirties their hands with the hard work of missions, whether at home or abroad, will ask this question.

Sometimes I even found myself reasoning with God. "God, we've been doing this for quite a while. We've made a difference. Couldn't we just go home? Couldn't I just get a real job and a real home, maybe one with a white picket fence near people who look and think like me? Wouldn't that be okay?" Every time I start to think like this, all I can see is the vision of the nations gathered around the throne of God at the end of time, singing, "Salvation be to our God. . . ." I know my family and I cannot, and will not, give up until we have spent our last breath to see this happen. Knowing where things go, knowing what happens, knowing victory waits in store for us if we don't give up in mission should drive us to give up our money, our homes, and our lives so the lost may know Him.

The vision of the end and the song of victory are meant to enliven and catalyze the Church in its purpose especially when the cost of mission seems to be a crushing weight beyond our ability to bear. When this Bold Song of Victory becomes the soundtrack of our lives, we will live our lives according to the vision of the future and not the fears of the present.

A HUMBLE SONG OF PRAISE

AFTER TAKING IN this profound song of victory, one wonders, what remains to be said or sung? Yet the song of victory eventually gives way to a second song, one of praise:

> All of the angels who had stood surrounding the throne and the elders and the four living creatures also fell before the throne upon their faces, and they worshipped God, saying:
>   It's true!
>   Blessing and glory and wisdom and thanksgiving and honor
>   and power and might be to our God, forever and ever!
>   It's true!
>
>   REVELATION 7:11–12

With a new song there also comes a new choir, or at least a greatly expanded choir. In this second song, the angels receive the focus of attention. The Greek verb *heistēkeisan* indicates all this time, through the last song and the scene involving the crowd of the redeemed, the angels have been standing, encircling the throne and, the crowd of the redeemed. We also learn the elders and living creatures have been present as the nearest of all to the throne.

Some scholars suggest only the angels will sing this second song. In such a case, after the crowd of the redeemed sings the Bold Song of Victory, the angels immediately respond by voicing their Humble Song of Praise. This reading makes sense on the face of things, since the grammar of the passage only explicitly places the words of the second song in the mouths of the angels themselves. However, I, along with others, would argue the image of concentric circles around the throne, moving from the outermost circle of the angels to the throne itself, expands the membership of the first choir of the redeemed rather than replacing it. Now the choir includes the redeemed *along with* all of the inhabitants of heaven. No being in all of the vast expanse of heaven will be able to keep from joining in on this second song.

More than just the exponential expansion of the choir, the second song somehow brings with it a fundamental change in posture and attitude. Recall the distinctiveness of the Bold Song of Victory. During this song, the choir had the audacity to stand boldly in the very presence of the living God—right in His throne room, of all places! Now the picture reverses. Instead of standing boldly and crying out a song of victory, the angels and the redeemed fall on their faces, and they worship.

The image of concentric rings strongly implies a kind of domino effect where each ring falls prostrate, followed by the succeeding rings, until no creature in all of heaven sees anything but pavement. Wow! What a contrast between verses 10 and 11. In the former, we beheld a triumphant throng, chins up, faces set. We could imagine the glory of the Lord reflecting off their faces. We could almost feel their confidence—not arrogance, not reliance on human sufficiency, not self-confidence, but God-confidence unalloyed with anything false. In the blink of an eye, inexplicably, all of this melts away, and not only do the redeemed lose the will to exercise their right to stand in God's presence, but no one anywhere remains upright. The obvious question is, what happened? What, in all the universe, could possibly cause the mood and posture of the ultimate worship service to shift so dramatically?

I believe the explanation for the radical change between the two songs has to do with the Christians of first-century Asia Minor being a lot like me. In many ways, my walk of faith has been more of a walk of doubt. Everything God ever promised me I have at some point doubted. I remember the specific moment I knew God called me to pursue a PhD. I determined to follow God in this call and promise. However, soon I started to think either God made a mistake, or I misheard Him. I questioned if I possessed the mental equipment necessary. I doubted.

One incident in particular renewed my conviction. In the first chapel service of a new semester the faculty clad in their academic robes prepared to march into the chapel. A friend and I were talking nearby when the professor who was the source of much of my first-semester doubts did something quite unexpected. He took off his doctoral cap and put it on my head. He said, "Chris, you're going to be wearing one of these someday." When Dr. McGee said these words, I knew I hadn't missed the message, nor had God made a mistake. Somehow, in that moment, doubt became faith once more.

A prophetic word from one of my most difficult teachers should have been quite a source of encouragement. However, though I graduated with my master's degree with a very high GPA, I quickly found myself rejected by both PhD. programs to which I applied. Again, I doubted. I enrolled in another master's level program, but the future was anything but certain. However, only six months into my second master's degree, I was accepted into the PhD. program at the University of Aberdeen in Scotland, one of the best schools in the world for New Testament studies.

Again, my faith soared. Then about a year into the program, I had a new baby and a 200-year-old flat I couldn't afford to keep warm. A weak U.S. dollar meant I possessed enough money for tuition and rent, but not for food. Daily I faced the agony and pressures of the British education system, in which everything comes down to an all-or-nothing oral examination of a thesis that students fail regularly. You can spend five years and $100,000 and walk away with student loan payments but no degree. Yes, I most certainly doubted whether we would survive those years and whether I would ever earn my degree. Without our even making a request, someone from our church started giving us enough money to buy groceries every month. My research went exceedingly well, beyond my or anyone's expectations, and I graduated in record time.

This little tale is not just a chronicle of my story; it echoes the story of everyone who tries to walk the walk of faith. All but supersaints (none of whom I have ever met and whose existence I strongly doubt) regularly pace a circuit between doubt and belief. If this can and does happen to us when we live in relative peace, safety, and freedom, how much more would it have happened to our first-century brothers and sisters who lived in Asia Minor?

Reading the letter of Revelation, they, like we, would have been awestruck by the beautiful, mysterious, and inspiring scenes which tell the Church where events will lead if we don't give up on mission. They would have read the Bold Song of Victory, and they likely would have responded something like this: "Yeah, John, you're right. If that's how things go, if that is what happens when we don't give up on mission, then it's worth it! Preaching the gospel with our words and with our lives is worth losing our money, our homes, and our lives. But wait a minute. How do we know the God who promised triumph can

> *How do we know He will keep His promise—or even if He can?*

really bring about this spectacular victory? How do we know He can really bring history to the place He said it will go? How do we know He will keep His promise — or even if He can?"

Remember, these folks were being asked to risk their lives, the lives of their children, and the lives of their spouses. They faced the distinct possibility of losing their homes and their jobs. At the end of the day, they ran the risk of no place to live or food to eat, and all because of their unwavering commitment to the gospel. For them, Revelation would have been an important source of comfort and encouragement with its promise of ultimate victory in the face of almost inconceivable opposition in mission. Still, from time to time, they would have doubted their ability to endure, God's ability to conquer, and even God's reliability in keeping His promises. How in the world could this promise of victory seem anything but pie-in-the-sky thinking on the worst of days and naive optimism on the best of days? This is why the second song is an absolute necessity. It is a song for the doubter in all of us.

The second song begins with the Hebrew word *amen*. You may have been surprised my translation rendered this word as "It's true!" Most Bibles simply leave it untranslated, as *amen*. The average Christian uses this word several times a day without ever thinking about what it actually means. When we pray and say "amen" at the end, what we really mean is, "may this thing become true." In some churches, people get excited during the sermon, and someone may shout, "Amen, brother!" or something similar. What they mean is, "Hey, what this guy is saying is true!"

Interestingly, this Humble Song of Praise begins and ends with the word *amen*—it's true. Of the fifty-nine times *amen* occurs in the entire Bible, only here does it come at the beginning and the end of a line of Scripture. In this case, *amen* forms the bookends of one of the two songs we know will be sung at the worship service to end all worship services. Just imagine the entire mind-blowingly huge, impossible-to-count throng of heaven shouting, "IT'S TRUE!" at the beginning and at the end of this song of praise while falling on their faces like dominoes. This unique scene declares to us, the readers, not only are the words of this song true, but they are truth itself. The words of this song declare the truth upon which the entire universe stands and holds together.

The lyrics between the *amens* concern themselves with a specific and fundamental truth—the nature and character of the God whom we serve. They form a recitation and revelation of the divine attributes, the characteristics that make God, God, and not something or someone else. John does not report a complete list of the divine attributes to us here, but rather a list designed to reassure the Church—the God who promised He would take all of history to a place of absolute unconditional victory can and will keep His promise to do so.

BLESSING

The first attribute to resonate throughout the heavens seems simple enough. Our God defines himself in terms of blessing and praise. More precisely, the choir declares Him to be the one who is above all others blessed and the object of praise. The Greek word *eulogia* has at its root the idea of "good" (*eu*) and "speech" (*logia*), and this constitutes praise — the speaking of good words concerning God and His deeds.

This attribute would have been greatly reassuring to the church in Asia Minor. They wondered whether the promise of victory could really be accomplished in the midst of their circumstances. Yet the blessed and praised nature of God reminds them there will never be, can never be, a time when those who understand the true nature of things will have anything but the best and highest things to say about our God. This could not be the case if He were a God who breaks His promises. A promise-breaking God would deserve ridicule and disdain, not blessing and praise.

GLORY

The song also imputes glory to God as one of His divine characteristics. This word "glory" (*doxa*) has such a rich and multifaceted meaning that only with great difficulty can we translate it into English. It concerns the manifest presence of God which brings with it a palpable weight and splendor that defies description, categorization, and human words. And no doubt this sense does apply to some degree, since this whole worship scene takes place in the manifest presence of the living God. Moreover, "glory" often has a meaning associated with the world to come after this one. Therefore, in a shorthand kind of way, "glory" evokes the world which all Christians long to see — a world which will become visible when history reaches its goal before the *glorious* throne of God on that day. The shadow of another world hangs in the air around "glory," but there is something more concrete we should not miss.

Glory can also be translated as "honor" or "reputation," and in the first-century Greco-Roman world of Asia Minor, this usage shows up often in reference to patron/client relationships. The typical first-century patron was very interested in attaining a good reputation by cultivating the arts and other honorable activities through his support of clients. Indeed, patrons often commissioned musical compositions not completely unlike the songs of Revelation. In gratitude for the support of their patrons, clients were obligated to declare the greatness, goodness, and wisdom of their patrons publicly and often.

Clients testified as character witnesses if their patrons faced any legal difficulties, and they could not testify against their patrons in court cases. Throughout the New Testament, one finds plenty of support for the idea God acts as a patron who cares for the needs of His clients (His people — the Church), but unlike worldly patrons, His care for them comes with no ulterior motives. He doesn't need their acclaim to enhance His reputation, status, or honor. Those things belong to Him as constituent elements of His very being. Instead, He genuinely has our best interests at heart when He provides for us everything we need. In loving and joyous response, with no thought of obligation or fear of losing future blessings, this Humble Song of Praise expresses the absolute loyalty of all creation to Him as their patron and provider.

Here the Humble Song of Praise declares the sterling reputation of our provider God. He is truly glorious, beyond the ear-popping peals of thunder, emerald thrones, shimmering rainbows, and seas of glass that often steal the show in Revelation. He gloriously provides for His children, and no matter what they suffer, the promise of victory rests on His good reputation as the Father and patron who never fails to give His dependents what they need. Thus, this song of praise sounded something like this to its first hearers: "Church in Asia Minor, in case you are wondering, know God's promise of victory cannot fail, because He has staked His reputation on it!"

WISDOM

Naturally, those doubting Christians of Asia Minor would have wondered whether God could possibly know enough to direct history to this culmination. Is God really smart enough to accomplish the promised victory? This doubt meets the response, "*Wisdom* be to our God!" In the Old Testament, wisdom usually refers to the ability to do something; it speaks of skill. In the Greek world, only the gods were thought to have true wisdom, in the sense of knowing comprehensively and with absolute precision the nature of things.

Revelation tends to be a curious fusion of Greco-Roman and Jewish thought patterns, and John likely intends a rather broad-spectrum concept of wisdom here. We can count on the coming victory because our God, Yahweh, knows the beginning, the end, and everything in between. He possesses absolutely perfect understanding of the nature and essence of things. More than just knowing *how* things are, He knows how to make His own plans and desires take shape. He has the skill which comes from perfectly and completely comprehending the nature of the universe. In other words, the promise of victory rests on the foundation of God's omniscience.

THANKSGIVING

As the song progresses from one character trait to another, we come to "thanks" or "thanksgiving." This one seems a little odd. Wisdom, glory, and blessing fit the mold of our expectations. We usually think of God in these exalted terms, but "thanks?" Does this mean God has thankfulness as one of His character traits? For what could He be thankful, and whom could He possibly thank besides himself? The answer probably does not lie along that path. Rather, part of God's nature consists of His being, someone to whom thanks is due. Of all the infinite attributes one could ascribe to God, this one, in spite of its strangeness, really does fit the purpose of this song perfectly.

Let me put it this way. Do we usually thank people who make promises they don't keep? Or do we feel a deep sense of gratitude when people offer us gifts we don't need? I don't know about you, but when people promise me things and then fail to deliver, I usually don't send thank-you notes. God is emphatically not like that. He does not make promises He does not keep, and He never gives white-elephant gifts. This song of praise reveals God to be, in the very fiber of His being, a God to whom thanks is due. When He makes a promise, He cannot fail to keep it. The promise of victory hangs on the certainty that we will thank God for victory one day because, due to His character and nature, He will not fail to bring about that which He has promised. Again, His character guarantees the future.

HONOR

Like thanksgiving, "honor" speaks of a God whose character backs up His promises. We do not usually consider folks honorable who make promises they don't keep. On the contrary, we usually call them scoundrels. Human nature despises the duplicity of people who say one thing and do another. This Humble Song of Praise declares our God is emphatically not like that. When He says a thing, He does the thing. All of Scripture reveals an honorable God who jealously guards His reputation. God relented from destroying Israel at Mount Sinai because of His honor (Ex. 32:12).

In Mediterranean culture, hardly any force had equal power to influence the thinking and behavior of people as shame and honor did. Nations went to war to protect their honor and to remove shame. Marriages, contracts, and all of the most important decisions in life had necessarily to take into account the honor and shame dynamic. If someone even accidentally shamed another, honor had to be satisfied, and often lives were lost in the defense of honor. God's honor reveals to us He will always and forever do right by His people. He will keep His promises, but more than just keeping promises, His character proves the shame of exile, execution, and poverty cannot endure. They cannot be the last word for the Church, because His character will not allow it.

So far, the Humble Song of Praise grounds the promise of victory in the magnificent integrity of God's character—His dependability so far transcends human experience it defies comparison. The nagging question? Does superior disposition and intention equate to ability? Sure, God wants to keep His promises, but can He really do it? Remember, Rome was pretty impressive—a city of one million people, an empire which covered the entire known world, a military no one could withstand, and a ruler who claimed to be a god.

POWER AND MIGHT

At its very climax, the song declares the "power" and "might" of the creator God. In the New Testament, "power" (*dunamis*) speaks of divine healing and the working of miracles (Luke 1:35, 5:17, 6:19). It also describes God's saving power (Acts 1:8 Rom. 1:16; 1 Cor. 1:18) and His creative power displayed throughout the world (Rom. 1:20). "Might" (*ischun*) probably does draw some attention to God's regal and kingly authority—His right and prerogative to treat absolutely everyone as a subordinate, but primary attention falls upon His ability.

To sing of God's might is to profess and proclaim He, by His very nature, has the ability to do all He promised to do. In other words, it speaks of His omnipotence. Can He really fulfill the promise of victory? You'd better believe it! He has all of the ability, authority, and wonder-working power to make that which He promises materialize before our eyes, in defiance of physics, probability, expectation, and anything else which seems to put a question mark over His Word.

When all of heaven realizes the promise of ultimate victory finds its root and ground in the very character of the God whom we serve, their only response can be to fall on their faces and to sing a Humble Song of Praise in which His characteristics receive the adoration due them. Best of all, the song ends with the declaration, "for ever and ever! *It's true!*" God's promises do not come with an expiration date or a statute of limitations.

> *God's promises do not come with an expiration date or a statute of limitations.*

Regardless how many centuries pass between the revelation of victory and the Church's possession of it, the promise cannot fail. It has an unlimited shelf life because it finds its root and foundation in the very nature and character of the unchanging God who holds the universe itself together.

For the Church weighing whether to risk their money, homes, and lives for the sake of mission, the Humble Song of Praise brings home the concrete nature of the promise. Indeed, in light of the grave dangers associated with it, mission only makes sense to whatever degree victory can be certain. Now no question remains. God guarantees victory by staking himself to it.

Mission carries the threat of severe temporary suffering, but in terms of ultimate outcome, God has rigged the game, and the odds are 100 percent in favor of absolute victory. However, as the whole letter of Revelation reminds its readers over and over again, those who compromise with the world, who abandon mission for the sake of prosperity, comfort, and safety in this world, disqualify themselves from partaking in the coming victory.

PRAISE: THE LEITMOTIF OF THE SOUNDTRACK OF OUR LIVES

WE HAVE ALREADY discussed how God intends for us as believers to make the Bold Song of Victory the soundtrack of our lives. We have looked into the power of this song to help us make sense of our own existence, anticipate the turns in our own stories, and frame those stories in the context of the grand drama of the universe unfolding according to God's plan. Allowing the Bold Song of Victory to structure the story of our lives gives us the spiritual resources to make practical decisions based on the promise of the future rather than the fears of the present. It's the vehicle by which we reify Christian convictions about the kingdom of God.

But living life on the basis of this song takes faith. The victory does lie in the future. The cost of missions in the present may indeed be very high. Acting upon what we know to be true in the absence of really seeing it physically precisely matches the definition of faith, or more accurately, faithfulness, provided by the author of the book of Hebrews. "Faithfulness is the concrete experience of the things for which we hope. Faithfulness is action that makes visible what otherwise could not be seen" (Heb. 11:1). Nonetheless, as we live by the rules of the future in the present, as the Bold Song of Victory beckons us to faithfulness, from time to time, doubt will enter our minds. Therefore, another musical theme is required. This, of course, is none other than the Humble Song of Praise. In musical terms, the song of praise functions as a leitmotif. Merriam-Webster offers this explanation of *leitmotif*:

> In opera, a leitmotif is a recurring melody that accompanies the reappearance of an idea, person, or situation. The term is now applied in other kinds of music, sometimes with a meaning very close to the original: "The Imperial March" that is heard in the *Star Wars* film franchise whenever Darth Vader appears on screen, for example, is a modern example of leitmotif.[10]

Star Wars has come back into the picture! However, this time, the blame lies with Merriam-Webster and not with me. The point is the praise of God and His attributes is the musical strain running through our soundtracks as we conduct our lives to the rhythm of the song of victory. The song of praise must do this, because as we cast aside all claim to our money, lives, and homes to pursue the mission God has given us to be His partners in

---

10. Merriam-Webster, s.v. "leitmotif," accessed September 10, 2020, https://www.merriam-webster.com/dictionary/leitmotif.

bringing salvation to the world, doubt and fear will come back to us again and again. Yet, each time they do, the leitmotif of praise intervenes to help us overcome them by tying our confidence of future victory to God's attributes — His character.

The churches in Asia Minor to whom John addressed Revelation needed the song of praise. Many of them were losing sight of the future through doubt, and they desperately needed to remember future victory isn't merely an ephemeral wish. Future victory has real substance because God has staked His reputation to it and guaranteed it by His character.

As I write this, our world is in the throes of the Coronavirus pandemic of 2020, and perhaps you have many reasons to doubt the future. Maybe you have seen loved ones die. Maybe the economic effects of the virus have disrupted or destroyed your plans and dreams for the future. Maybe God has given you a calling and made promises to you that now seem beyond all possibility of fulfillment. Global upheavals like the one we're living through, and perhaps worse ones to come, naturally bring with them doubt about the future. In truth, whether we will admit it or not, times such as these often cause us to doubt God. Indeed, in the face of such crises, doubts about God's promises, doubts about His wisdom, and especially doubts about His power to produce ultimate victory inevitably rise.

In the Church, we are often afraid of doubt. After all, aren't we supposed to be people of faith and not doubt? Yes! But, understand faith requires the possibility of doubt. In the absence of really good reasons to doubt, we do not *need* faith. In other words, faith and doubt are not polar opposites. Rather, doubt constitutes the necessary precondition for faith. It is only in an atmosphere full of doubt, faith can really thrive and grow. Take Abraham for example, when God promised him he would have a son by Sarah, he doubted. He laughed and asked God if a man 100 years old could really have a child with a woman of 90? Then he made a suggestion to God. Why not just bless Ishmael (Gen. 17:17–18)?

Note Abraham and Sarah's bodies were worn out and incapable of producing offspring. They did not deny the truth of this for one moment. Instead, they chose to act on the basis of the future God promised. God promised to build a nation from the offspring of two old people who were as good as dead (Heb. 11:12). Even though he had every reason to doubt, and even though he did actually doubt, Abraham walked the path of obedience. This is faith! Faith is acting on the future at the very moment when there seems to be no future. Why did Abraham keep obeying in spite of his doubts? To answer this question, we have to look to the covenant God made with him.

Faith is acting on the future at the very moment when there seems to be no future.

> He said to him, "I am the LORD who brought you out from Ur of the Chaldeans to give you this land to possess." But he said, "O Lord GOD, how am I to know that I shall possess it?" He said to him, "Bring me a heifer three years old, a female goat three years old, a ram three years old, a turtledove, and a young pigeon." And he brought him all these, cut them in half, and laid each half over against the other. But he did not cut the birds in half. And when birds of prey came down on the carcasses, Abram drove them away. . . .
>
> **When the sun had gone down and it was dark, behold, a smoking fire pot and a flaming torch passed between these pieces** [Gen. 15:7–11, 17 ESV; emphasis added].

At the very peak of doubt, when Abraham couldn't see how God's promise of descendants or a land could be realized, Genesis 15 reinforces the security of the future based on God's character.

At the climax of the scene unfolding in Genesis 15, the manifest presence of God, in the form of fire, passes between animals which had been cut in half. Usually, this ceremony sealed an agreement between two parties. Each party would walk between the carcasses of the slain animals and thereby cement a solemn oath. However, in this case, only God passes between the animals. This shows the promises God has made depend completely on His own character, without reference to external factors such as biology, politics, or human weakness.

The animals too have great importance. They have been slaughtered and cut in half to invoke a kind of curse. The one who makes an oath by walking through the pieces of dead flesh says, in effect, "If I break my promise, may I be slaughtered and cut asunder like these animals." In other words, the oath maker stakes his reputation, character, and even his life on his promise. In the face of Abraham's overwhelming doubts about the future, God reveals His character. Yahweh himself shows the patriarch the promised future is guaranteed because it rests on God's own character traits — the same character traits celebrated in the Humble Song of Praise, namely, blessing, wisdom, honor, thanks, and power.

In missions, reasons to doubt abound in times such as ours. If you don't believe me, just consider the last worldwide pandemic. In 1918–1920, the deadly Spanish Flu pandemic ravaged the world. It killed at least 50 million people. During those years filled with danger, quarantine, and economic hardship, the Assemblies of God did not shrink back one bit in their zeal to evangelize the never-reached people of Asia Pacific and the world. In particular, let me introduce you to some missionaries who served in Fiji during difficult days not unlike those we face in 2020. Meet Albert and Lou Page.

The Pages were filled with the Holy Spirit in 1911 and were the first Assemblies of God missionaries to Fiji.[11] In the beginning, their living conditions were very difficult. In a letter published in the *Christian Evangel*, Albert describes his family's hardships in graphic detail.

> Our living was exceedingly poor, sometimes reduced to $1.00 per week ($25.90 in 2020). Trials were many and at times we could not appear in public owing to our scanty and worn out attire. Our dwelling places of the past were grass houses and often the rain would pour in on us in bed.[12]

In other letters, Albert describes trekking through the wilderness for days in the pouring rain and being soaked the entire time in order to take the gospel to the never reached. In spite of everything he and his family endured, the Fijians were very slow in coming to faith. Many times, in desperation and at their wits' end, parents would bring sick children and relatives to the Pages for prayer. God answered their prayers with healing, but the Pages lamented that, in spite of the miracles, the Fijians often did not turn to God.[13]

Eventually, the Pages found great success in their evangelistic efforts, but they also came to realize the deeper spiritual reality

---

11. Norman S. Farrington, "Eight Generations Baptized in the Sprit," in *Assemblies of God Heritage* (2001), vol. 21, no. 2, 27; Rosemarie Daher Kowalski, "What Made Them Think They Could?: Ten Early Assemblies of God Female Missionaries," in *Assemblies of God Heritage* (2014), vol. 34, 71.

12. "Bro. and Sister Page" in *The Christian Evangel*, April 6 (1918), 11.

13. "Bro. Albert T. Page" in *The Christian Evangel*, May 4 (1918), 11.

behind their sufferings and difficulties. Albert explains the lesson they learned:

> We suffered many hardships and were face to face with death many times traveling in the wild places. Scores of souls found the Lord, but still we were yet in school. We could tell the people of Jesus and His blood, but we were no match for the warfare put up against us by Satan.[14]

In saying this, Albert doesn't in any way suggest Satan is stronger than God or Satan can stop the mission of the Church to evangelize the world. Rather, he is looking back on all of the trials and hardships he has undergone and can detect how, through them, God had trained him and his wife to fight the schemes of Satan and to do the work of evangelism.

Anyone who reads the Pages' reports can sense their passion and radical otherworldliness. They had left their money and comfortable home behind to live in a leaky grass hut with their four children on $1 per week. In their reports, among the trials, the glimmering gold of fruitful and joyful obedience shines through. I can think of no clearer example of a family whose life story had been scored to the Bold Song of Victory. Still, all was not victory for them.

As the Pages' ministry entered its greatest period of effectiveness and fruitfulness, Albert traveled widely, preaching and working diligently to prepare native Fijians to minister. During this same time, the influenza broke out in Suva, Fiji's capital. Albert did not think about the virus in terms of danger, but in terms of opportunity to minister. Seizing the opportunity afforded by the scourge of the pandemic, "he went to one of the temporary

---

14. "Bro. Albert T. Page" in *The Christian Evangel*, July 27 (1918), 10.

hospitals to do night work to help the suffering ones."[15] Having already given up money and home for the sake of mission, this last step of obedience would cost Albert his life. While ministering to those sick with the flu, Albert soon became ill, and on December 9, 1918, he took his place among the multitude of worshippers surrounding the throne of God.

Lou Page's next communication to the readers of the *Christian Evangel* began with these heart-rending words: "I suppose you received a wire announcing the death of my husband, Albert T. Page."[16] If there was ever a moment to doubt, it had come. After Albert's death, Lou Page felt overwhelmed. She seriously doubted whether she could continue to care for four children and do all the missions work she and her husband had started together. She wrote to her supporters: "Please pray for me. I am left all alone with four little children. The conflict has been great, but thus far I have the victory thru the Blood. I intend to stay on here until I am sure of the Lord's leading, and meanwhile shall do all I can for the spread of the gospel."[17]

The next update from Fiji, written not by sister Page but by Sarah Dowie, read:

Your letter received today, just six days after dear Sister Page fell asleep in Jesus. She had influenza. As soon as Bro. Page died she sent for me to come and stay with her, but I was unable to go at that time. But Sister Page sent for me again, so I was with her, held her in my arms and comforted her, and later closed her eyes and prepared her for burial, as there is no undertaker here.[18]

15. "Sister Lou Page of Nadroga, Fiji," in *The Christian Evangel*," March 8 (1919), 10.
16. "Nadroga" in *The Christian Evangel*," February 22 (1919), 10.
17. Ibid., 10.
18. "Sister Lou Page Asleep in Christ," in *The Christian Evangel*, May 3 (1919), 10.

It is the Bold Song of Victory with its promise of triumph and the fruit of souls which inspires missionary courage to leave money and homes, and even to give up life itself, in the cause of Christ. When doubt assails us, as it will, what can keep us walking the difficult road of obedience? What keeps a family of six sleeping under a leaky grass roof? What keeps a missionary preaching when no one believes? What keeps him on the field when he can't afford clothing? What keeps him serving the afflicted when he knows that service is a death sentence? The vision of future victory impels those who would embrace the missional life to risk everything, but what holds us in place when all we can see is defeat?

In the same 1919 volume of the *Christian Evangel* in which the notice of Lou Page's death had appeared, another potential seed of doubt reared its ugly head. Elsewhere in Asia Pacific, missionaries in my own land of calling, Japan, also faced the doubts and suffering of those pandemic years. Marie Juergensen, who loved and taught many children in Tokyo, related this story about a young girl from her Sunday school.

One of my dear little Sunday School girls who I know loved Jesus and never failed to come to Sunday School whether it rained or snowed, died with influenza the other day. I remember so well her bright face as she told me how she prayed to Jesus. I am rejoicing in the blessed privilege of leading these little lambs to Jesus. Oh how I do love them all, and love the sweet gatherings we have together! It makes me greatly rejoice when I think that this dear little girl has gone to be with Jesus, because she learned to pray and love Jesus in our little Sunday School. I remember a few Sundays before she was taken sick, asking the children, "Who is Jesus?" One tiny fellow said, "Teacher, He is the one with the white clothes on."

(Many times in the pictures rolls Jesus is dressed in white.) Then another one said, "He is the One who heals sick people." Then I saw this little girl raise her hand, (the only one who had her hand up in the whole room), and she answered, "He is the true God of Heaven."[19]

Could not the true God of heaven have protected this little girl? Though Sister Juergensen did not ask this question, you can bet it came into her heart at some point. Every time and everywhere Jesus' followers choose to bet everything on the future, the doubts of the present threaten to eclipse our view of what is to come. In John's day, the might and fury of imperial Rome occluded the Church's view of the future—leaving them stumbling in the darkness of doubt. A hundred years ago, war, famine, economic catastrophe, and global pandemic shrouded the future. Is God really strong enough? Is He really smart enough? Does He really keep His promises? In the face of such doubts, how did Marie Juergensen and the Pages remain faithful?

To really get at the heart of this question, we need to hear the voice of a missionary to India, where the Spanish influenza hit with the greatest ferocity. Between 1913 and 1918, the cost of goods in India doubled, imposing great hardship on common people. Then a crop failure in 1918 led to severe famine. Left physically weak and vulnerable by these hardships, when the flu pandemic arrived, the people of India had no strength to fight the virus, and between 14 and 17 million died. Among those were several Assemblies of God missionaries. Those missionaries who survived nearly worked themselves to death caring for the sick and hungry multitudes. Living daily with suffering on such a scale

---

19. "Tokio," in *The Christian Evangel*, May 3 (1919), 10.

was indeed a heavy burden to carry. Under such circumstances, anyone could easily doubt or lose sight of the future. Yet, we find the secret to survival and continued faithfulness in the words of an unnamed missionary:

> Once when the agony was so great that it seemed I would die the Lord said to me, "Smile". I could hardly believe it was His voice, but He very tenderly went on to show me that I was to rejoice and be exceedingly glad for the wonderful privilege of entering into the fellowship of His sufferings. I smiled and believe it saved me from a complete nervous breakdown. After that when the agony became too great to bear I simply raised my face to Heaven and smiled. This may sound crazy to you, but it is a fact.[20]

In this missionary's response, one can hear a heart of thankful praise to God that leads to joy in the midst of the unbearable. Indeed, hints of this attitude come through in the Pages' updates, in which they regularly express thanks for God's grace and His provision—His promise-keeping character. You can hear the same thing in the of heart of praise behind Marie Jurgensen's rejoicing for the opportunity of leading little ones to Christ in spite of the fact she lost one to the flu.

Obedience to God's call to the missional life will bring with it moments of doubt—moments when our present difficulties and sufferings cause us to lose sight of the future triumph revealed in the Bold Song of Victory. For those moments, God has given us the Humble Song of Praise. God has designed praise to be the leitmotif of the soundtracks of our lives. Whenever the clouds of doubt and fear hide the future, praise reminds us God's character

---

20. "Amid India's Plague and Famine," in *The Christian Evangel*, February 22 (1919), 10.

guarantees the future. As a consequence, the closer we walk with Him, the more we know His Word, the more we are familiar with Him and His ways, the quicker the Humble Song of Praise springs to our lips in those dark moments of fear and doubt.

Perhaps COVID-19, the pandemic of 2020, has been or is one of those moments of doubt for you. Perhaps you are reading this from the other side of the pandemic's shadow but under another pall of blackness that hides the future. In the grip of doubt and fear, you, like the first-century Christians of Asia Minor, may feel the missional life just costs too much at the moment because you can't clearly see the future that makes it all worthwhile. I ask you to pause for a moment and consider God's character. Consider the fact God ties His reputation to the future — guaranteeing it with everything He is. As you do . . . why not just sing this little song? In fact, sing it as often as you need to.

> *It's true!*
>> *Blessing and glory and wisdom and thanksgiving and honor*
>>> *and power and might be to our God, forever and ever!*
>> *It's true!*

REREADING REVELATION AND RETHINKING MISSION

SO FAR in our time together, we have seen Revelation addresses a church in the midst of a crisis in mission and with every word, its message beckons the Church to risk everything for the sake of the never reached. Revelation is practical, not theoretical. The vision of the future changes our lives as Christians in the present. When mission costs our money, our homes, and our lives, the future calls out to us, "The cost is worth paying!" As the message of Revelation sinks deeply in our souls, we start to act on the promise of the future rather than the fears of the present.

Thus far, we have unpacked four verses containing two songs which put the message of Revelation into proper perspective. As we have now seen repeatedly, these songs address the churches of Asia Minor in the midst of a crisis in mission. The Bold Song of Victory imparts a vision of the future meant to inspire those first-century Christians to count their money, homes, and lives as expendable commodities in the task of missions. Revelation also recognizes that "all in" missions will lead to moments of darkness and doubt. Thus, the Humble Song of Praise is the leitmotif that repeatedly reminds every missional person God's character guarantees the future. Yet, what does it really mean to live life in 2020 and beyond with these songs as the soundtrack of our lives? In other words, how do we actually apply Revelation to our lives as modern Christians?

It is precisely here, where the rubber meets the road, many readings of Revelation fall flat. So, Russia is the bear to north, and there is a giant computer called "the Beast" in Europe clandestinely and insidiously collecting information on all of us. (Maybe we should call the internet "spawn of the Beast!") What should we do? Even if you really believed these conjectures, all of which were in vogue when I was kid growing up in church, you probably did nothing about it.

The Cold War created fear, and Christians turned to Revelation for answers, but the impulse of that time, as has often been the case, was for many readers to turn toward allegorical applications of Revelation's strange and ancient symbols to modern problems and personages—whether it be attack helicopters or the Pope. I will not spend effort debunking such theories; time has already done that work. It will do its work on many current theories; the crises and beasts will, in all probability, pass without incident just as the year 2000 did.

The danger, however, lies in the fact speculation domesticates the message of Revelation; the minutia swallows the mandate, and prophecy becomes a hobby safely isolated from the real world, without any power to challenge us, much less to change us. With the emphasis on the prophetic and the end times we find capturing the imagination of the Church during the current pandemic, we must recognize both danger and opportunity.

One danger lies in the repetition of history. Creative bloggers and popular preachers daily make predictions, trying to connect the current political situation, health problems, legal decisions, and religious climate to the chapters of Revelation. I decline to take up specific theories or address the historical and exegetical merits of the various proposals here. If they happen to guess right about the timing of the end and the persons and events involved, I will be happy to rejoice with them as we gather together around the throne. However, it is possible to perfectly decode Revelation and still miss the point. We miss the point when the Church gets caught up in the thrill of speculation, and in so doing, never asks what kind of Christian life the end of the world demands.

Lest you think me to be some kind of overintellectualized prophetic humbug, let me emphasize I do see great opportunity in the present moment of prophetic interest. The Church has many good reasons to be turning to Revelation and thinking of the end just now. Whenever the Church is in this mood, Revelation can do its work of reframing our worldviews and our priorities according to that which truly matters. Indeed, Revelation's missional message has the potential to enliven and empower the Church. It has the potential to be the big, red reset button which reframes reality, so we know how to understand the times in which we're living. More than that, it has the potential to teach us what concrete actions fit our times. In other words, moments such as the present one are great opportunities for Revelation's songs to once again become the soundtrack of our lives, just as they were always meant to be.

I would like to suggest the church in North America and throughout the world is facing a crisis in mission not unlike the one that faced the first-century church in Asia Minor. Perhaps no government officials plan to confiscate our property, send believers into exile, or murder the faithful — at least in the West. However, forces in our world, such as culture, present a challenge no less dangerous than an armed Roman cohort was to the Early Church. Hard choices still have to be made by those who would be followers of Christ. Looking into the situation of the seven churches, we see when confronted with the cost of truly missional living, Christians respond in three basic ways. We either denounce, domesticate, or embrace mission. So, lets look at what denouncing, domesticating, and embracing might look like, for both those who go and those who send, from a 2020 American perspective.

GOERS

It used to be only a strange, select, and in the minds of some, elite group of people fit the description of "missionary." Folks who would make a commitment, leave friends, family, and home, and spend the majority of their lives laboring in far-off places. However, times have changed. Missionaries do not travel in boats for months to get to the field. Indeed, for relatively little cost, one can board a plane and be anywhere on the planet within twenty-four hours. Many churches send members on short-term trips, and many full-time missionaries spend a block of years overseas, and then return home. Missions, in the traditional sense of those who cross a cultural and geographic boundary to spread the gospel, has expanded in our age and become part of the lives of more believers than ever. Nonetheless, even in a church full of goers, the challenge of Revelation bids us to reflect carefully on what it means to be a fully missional church.

DENOUNCING

Like the first-century church to which the letter of Revelation was written, strong cultural and economic forces in our world threaten to diminish and even extinguish the urgency of mission in our own day. Culturally, we live in an age of relativism. I do not wish to start beating the drum about the dangers of postmodernism; this has been done quite often enough by authors who are more philosophically astute than me. Obviously, the exclusive truth claims which occupy a central position in Christian belief cannot easily assimilate postmodern notions of tolerance and relativism. Here, I am talking broadly about the commonly held idea that we as Christians, or anyone else, for that matter, can only talk about what is true for us. We are told we cannot talk about Truth with a capital *T*, since no truth applies to everyone. Some may feel a missions movement such as the Assemblies of God is immune to such thinking. I don't think we can be too sure of that.

Even the most staunchly evangelical branches of the worldwide Church are beginning to reap the missiological fruit of postmodernism. It isn't that our fellow evangelicals really question the saving power of Jesus or the necessity of believing in Him and living for Him. Rather, the effects come subtly and largely afflict the younger generations. We don't disbelieve the truth of the gospel, but we doubt our right to impose our belief on others. No matter how firmly convinced we are of Jesus being the way *for us*, we balk at the arrogance of claiming He is the way *for others*. This line of thinking threatens mission at its very core and has the potential to slowly cool missional zeal even for the likes of us.

No conspiracy or blatantly antimissional teaching bears the blame for the impending missional ice age. For many, their discomfort with aggressive mission never enters the conscious mind. It is a latent and unnoticed line of code programmed into the recesses of the mind as part of our cultural operating system by countless television shows, movies, teachers, and informal conversations with friends. Yet, it could cause the baton of mission to be dropped as it passes from one generation to another. Interestingly enough, part of the danger lies in the possibility that when the baton does fall, no one will even notice.

Let me explain what I mean. Very probably, the future of the evangelical church in the United States and other Western countries will not look much different in terms of domestic mission than it does today. Many of the unsaved in these parts of the world do not really convert from something else to Christianity. Instead, their past religious lives often entail little more than a vague sense of spirituality, and the evangelical church rightly does and (I predict) will continue to do much to attract and evangelize them (though its methods will no doubt change).

The danger lies with those who have been happily engaged in the traditional faiths of their forefathers for generation after generation. What of the Buddhists, Hindus, and Muslims of the world? Will the Church of the future still call them lost? Will they still send laborers to convert them? Fewer and fewer Christians believe faith in Jesus is the *only* path to salvation. In extreme cases, they might say, "Christ is my choice" or "Jesus is the best of the many available options." Even a slight shift toward pluralism will destroy the Church's global sense of mission. Reckless abandonment to the task of evangelizing the world cannot survive if we entertain even a shadow of a doubt.

As with the church in first-century Asia Minor, so cultural pressure threatens to cause us to denounce mission. However, our choice will not likely be between Christianity or idolatry. Rather, it will be a choice between a tolerant, gutted, missionally anemic faith that timidly declares Jesus to be the answer *for me* and the robust Church of mission that has been the vanguard of Kingdom advancement in past centuries. If I have been reading Revelation rightly, the difference between these two paths is no small matter. Indeed, from the perspective of the Apocalypse, taking the path away from missional zeal puts one in danger of being eternally damned. I am aware this seems harsh, but the path of compromise that would blunt and then destroy the faith looks exactly like this in Revelation. Mission takes a backseat to safety and cultural acceptance, and because mission lies near the heart of the Christian faith, soon nothing identifiably Christian remains.

Economic factors today pose essentially the same threat they did two millennia ago. We see that for the church reading Revelation, concern for possessions carried with it the power to kill mission. As the pandemic wreaks havoc on the global economy on a scale not seen since the Great Depression, the economic threat to mission seems more relevant than ever. For the past several decades, our Western way of doing missions has been one entirely unknown to the first-century church. It has been a mission of abundance, in which sending missionaries did not, for the most part, directly impinge on one's standard of living. Missionaries themselves have often been sent with support ensuring a lower-middle-class lifestyle and adequate retirement.

Honestly, as someone who began his missionary career in such a system, I am grateful missions has only been a relative sacrifice for my family; but as resources become scarcer, both senders and goers may have to face the same choice the church in Asia Minor faced. Will we remain a Church and a people of mission when doing so means living well below our means and below our desired social status? As the Church wrestles with these questions, we would do very well to consider the message of Revelation and consider where things end up if we will only stay the course when it comes to mission. The time has come to behave as if this world truly has nothing for us. It is time to bet everything on the world to come.

DOMESTICATING

What does it look like today when those who go either consciously or unconsciously domesticate the radical missiology of Revelation? The churches who read the letter of Revelation had to be willing to lose their homes in order to remain churches of mission. Obviously, in their case, without suffering the loss of home, there would have been no multiethnic choir around the throne. However, what happens when missionaries leave home without ever *really* leaving?

One can go to another country without ever abandoning home in heart. In such cases, cultural values, forms of worship, financial behaviors, leadership methods, and a host of other things become gospel stowaways. The home-hearted missionary preaches a gospel which transforms his environment into an inevitably poor copy of his country of origin. For evidence of this, one need only see firsthand the many missions compounds around the world that function like small American towns in the midst of decidedly non-American environments. Or one could survey the many church buildings standing out like bad architectural jokes in the midst of pagodas, grass huts, yurts, and high rises. Perhaps more tellingly, I've attended countless Asian church services featuring music borrowed from the West, only the lyrics have been translated. Nothing distinctive of a people uniquely created by God to worship Him peeks through. Although those who study missions have written volumes on the need to incarnate the gospel into the cultures of the world, practice lags behind because missionaries find it exceedingly difficult to leave home behind.

Unfortunately, the Xerox brand of missions produces a fair share of success stories. How could it fail when the poor desperately desire to be like the rich? This is domestication, but what if the untamed gospel were allowed to run wild through the savannahs of Africa, the rice paddies of Asia, and the ice fields of Siberia? Church would probably not be comfortable for Westerners. The difference between cultural forms and true Christianity would be painfully exposed. Daughter churches with theology different than mother churches would cause some suffering and a lot of deep thinking among Western "parents." Mission would be a messy and uncomfortable business. Yet, the song sung by the nations around the throne at the end of time reminds those of us who go that the pain of utterly losing all things "home" for the sake of the gospel is but a small price to pay.

EMBRACING

Those goers who fully embrace the vivid and clarion call of the Apocalypse toward a missional existence will be radicals who courageously leave behind opportunities for financial security, abandon the comfort of their homes, and even risk their lives so the world may know Christ. A clear vision of the end will not allow them to be timid or relativistic in preaching the gospel as the only path to eternal life. Their allegiance will be to another world and another kingdom. They will not be afraid to be ambassadors of an untamed gospel that inspires local bodies of believers to express themselves in new and exciting ways that constantly expand the dimensions of the worship directed to our God and King. They will have truly abandoned home for the sake of the gospel. Some will experience plenty, others will know want in their fields of service, but they will live generous and satisfied lives because they are rooted in the future rather than the present. These are those who look beyond the world that is and see the world to come.

SENDERS

Most Christians will either never cross cultural and geographic boundaries in mission, or they will do so only temporar- ily. However, they still have a vital and life-long role to play in mission as senders. One can easily talk about being radical and risking life and limb to carry the gospel to the far corners of the world, but what does it mean to be a missional radical who never departs from the motherland?

DENOUNCING

It takes little imagination to visualize what happens when send- ers give up in mission. They don't pray the Lord of the harvest would raise up laborers for the harvest field. They don't train young people to cross oceans and preach the gospel, and they cer- tainly don't make financial sacrifices for the sake of winning the lost. In short, they either stop or never start the activity of sending out workers who will do the hands-on labor of planting and nur- turing the gospel in foreign lands. Does this seem far-fetched, at least for evangelicals?

I serve in a fellowship founded as a missionary-sending force. Indeed, the history of the Assemblies of God testifies to our com- mitment to this purpose. Although we have only a century of his- tory behind us, we have grown from nothing in 1914 to a global movement of nearly 70 million people today. Yet, as I call on churches in this "missions movement" to book missions services, occasionally the pastor will say, "We're not a missions church." I'm not whining. The Assemblies of God is awesome. I count it a privilege to be part of it, and I feel nothing but gratitude for all those churches and individuals who have supported my family as we have labored in the Philippines and Japan. Still, I insist we can't be complacent. It cannot be taken for granted the heart of our movement will always beat for missions.

I believe churches and individuals pass up the biblical mandate of sending missionaries for three primary reasons: finances, distrust of missions institutions, and theological misgivings. When it comes to finances, some churches believe they can't make a difference because of their lack of material resources. They feel the work of sending laborers should be left to bigger, richer congregations. The recent global economic meltdown has only exacerbated this situation, leading others to feel they don't have enough left over to contribute to missions.

Interestingly enough, recent studies have suggested the larger a church grows, the less generous it becomes per capita. Naturally, with sprawling campuses, dozens of staff pastors, and the trappings of the megachurch, ministry overhead increases dramatically. This brings us to the other side of the financial issue. Lack does not always explain the absence of missional zeal. Sometimes churches intentionally put all of their capital into domestic ministry in order to become the most attractive option for the fickle and mobile consumer Christians of the West. So, both lack and abundance can draw would-be senders away from mission.

Another factor we cannot afford to overlook is people who don't trust the missionary sending institutions. Sometimes the administrative costs, high salaries of executives, lack of financial transparency, and/or general mistrust of highly bureaucratic systems make people think twice about getting involved in sending missionaries. All missions organizations are full of people and are, therefore, imperfect; but we can't throw out the baby with the bathwater. We can, however, demand transparency, choose agencies understanding their strengths and weaknesses, and work for efficiency and integrity from the inside. At the end of the day, we couldn't deal with people at all if we expected perfection from any human organization, be it our banks, our governments, or our missions boards.

Finally, some refrain from sending missionaries because of their theology. I won't rehash what we've already explored about postmodernism and the gospel of Jesus as the answer *for me*. However, just as such a theology keeps Christians from going as missionaries, so it makes them uncomfortable with the idea of sending others to convert the Buddhists and Muslims of the world. Here too, the radical missiology of Revelation instructs us. For the most part, we have dwelt on the positive side of the songs in Revelation chapter 7, but we cannot ignore what failure in mission looks like in the Apocalypse. This letter closes with the unforgettable images of the great white throne judgment and the lake of fire, which await those who do not measure up (Rev. 20). Tolerance is not respect. Tolerance is negligent disregard for those in danger.

> *Tolerance is not respect. Tolerance is negligent disregard for those in danger.*

DOMESTICATING

Just as senders can abdicate their responsibility, so they can domesticate the radical missiology of sending found in the

Apocalypse. The vision of the end beckons us to treat our money, homes, and lives with contempt for the sake of the gospel. Very few Christians today realize this radical, apocalyptic missiology in real life. For most, sending will go no further than the financial dimension, and even within the purely monetary aspect of mission, few approach the sacrificial giving described in the book of Revelation. If I am at all on target with my reading of Revelation, a sense of mission which impels people to contribute only when things go well and abundance permits is by no means adequate.

Radical mission puts sending ahead of eating, insurance, and certainly before luxuries. Anything less is domestication. Lest you think I'm bashing those who support me and other missionaries and trying to manipulate people into giving, permit me to explain. Revelation essentially seeks to shock us into the realization this world and the things that look like success in it are an illusion and of no lasting value. John did not, and I do not, wish to make you neglect your family or your responsibilities. I want you to understand the danger of confusing the illusion with reality, the temporal with the eternal, the insignificant with the significant.

Senders also domesticate mission when they support missions as a substitute for doing missions. Mission is emphatically not the private territory of foreign missionaries. Each of us has a sphere of influence, and we have a divine mandate to proclaim Jesus with our words and our lives within that sphere. Ideally, being senders should heighten our concern for the souls of the lost who dwell halfway around the world and, at the same time, increase our concern for the lost who live across the street. No amount of support or payment erases our personal responsibility to respond to the Great Commission.

EMBRACING

Let's dream together about what it would look like for the senders of the world to embrace apocalyptic missiology. It would mean churches consciously and purposefully build simpler, more functional, and inexpensive facilities for the purpose of sending missionaries. We wouldn't take on mortgages that sap every last available cent and preclude the possibility of furthering our missions commitment. Individuals and families who embraced this radical missiology would not buy extra homes, speedboats, and extravagant vacations, choosing instead to make a more lasting investment. The less affluent might fast from Starbucks or drinking soda so they could make the same kind of investment.

Truly radical senders will have a missiology that lays down both home and life, but how do those who never leave home or die for the sake of the gospel give up their homes or lives? In today's Western culture, people have made a study of isolating and insulating themselves from the world around them. More than a few have elected to function as virtual social animals — living mostly through screens. Admittedly, this has become a necessity imposed on us to some extent during the days of COVID-19. Still, even before the pandemic, more and more, our homes had taken on the quality of a kind of inner sanctum into which only a select few may penetrate. We carefully select those with whom we will share our lives — ensuring their Facebook profiles suggest at least a modicum of shared interests.

I would like to suggest part of being a radically missional person who lays down home and life for the sake of the gospel should involve being uncomfortably open with one's home and life. It means having folks over for dinner often, making friends with people not because they have something to offer you but because they need to know Jesus. It means being transparent, approachable, and countercultural. It will not be easy, but those who don't give up will find themselves in the company of many friends one day gathered around the throne of God, voices raised together, singing the Bold Song of Victory.

CONCLUSION

AS YOU LEAVE the pages of this book, I hope you will take a few things with you. First, I want you to walk away encouraged. Whatever you are facing in your life which feels like it has the power to crush you, whatever feels like it could knock any breath of missional zeal out of you, know it cannot win. The promise of the song of victory is for you. Allow its message to reframe the way you see the world and your life. If you do, your problems will begin to look very small, and your God will begin to look very BIG. The result will be you find encouragement and strength to keep doing what God has created and called you to do. You will suddenly find yourself living life according to a new soundtrack, and your actions will not be dictated by the fears of the present; instead, you will make conscious and intentional decisions based on the promise of the future.

Second, if we really get the message of Revelation, the entire way we look at missions will change. Indeed, we will become radical in mission, to the point of being willing to give up our money, our homes, and our lives. This kind of apocalyptic missiology was the force that breathed life into the missions explosion of the early twentieth century, which marked the beginning of the Assemblies of God. Our spiritual forebears, such as the Pages who served in Asia Pacific, had no compunction about abandoning all so the never-reached people of Fiji and the world might know Christ. They believed the time was short before the Lord would split the eastern sky and return for His bride, the Church.

Whatever we may say about the nearly 100 years that have passed since they began their work, without Christ yet returning, they had the right idea. Theirs was an apocalyptic missiology, and so ours should be. The book of Revelation *is not* a call to date setting or abandoning life in society, but it *is* a call to live missional lives driven by a vision of the end. For those early Pentecostals, it meant doing things like trading their gold wedding rings for ones made of gunmetal and using the profits to send missionaries. They had little in worldly terms, but they were willing to bet the farm on the world to come.

Now we have come full circle. Yes, times are hard, and no one can see where the future of the world and its governments may lead. Naturally and rightly, we desire to find answers in the pages of the Apocalypse. Yet, beware of answers that don't cost anything—secret knowledge that changes nothing. I pray the Church turning to Revelation would, in these days, see a vision of the end that will propel it in mission. Then, our present health, economic, and political crises might just change the world.

Jesus walked this earth for exactly 40 days after His resurrection. During those 40 days one word resounds: GO. Dive into the stories and perspectives of people who love the never reached as they unpack why Jesus' words mandate all Christ-followers to Go.

ORDER

GO: A 40-DAY JOURNEY TO THE NEVER REACHED

and other great missions resources at
https://asiapacificmissions.org/neverreached

.